Word Accent in Japanese and English

What Are the Differences?

Miyoko Sugito

Translator **Hinako Masuda**
Supervisor **Donna Erickson**

HITUZI
SYOBO

Copyright © 2012 Miyoko Sugito
Japanese edition published 2012
English translation published 2014

Author: Miyoko Sugito
Professor Emeritus, Osaka Shoin Women's University

Translator: Hinako Masuda
Assistant Professor, Waseda University

Supervisor: Donna Erickson
Adjunct Faculty, Sophia University & Kanazawa Medical University

All rights reserved. Except for the quotation of short passages for the purposes of criticism and review, no part of this publication may be reproduced, stored in a retrieval system, or transmitted in any form or by any means, electronic, mechanical, photocopying, recording or otherwise, without the written prior permission of the publisher.
In case of photocopying and electronic copying and retrieval from network personally, permission will be given on receipts of payment and making inquiries. For details please contact us through e-mail. Our e-mail address is given below.

Cover designer: Fumi Watanabe

Hituzi Syobo Publishing
Yamato bldg. 2F, 2-1-2 Sengoku Bunkyo-ku Tokyo, Japan
112-0011

phone +81-3-5319-4916 fax +81-3-5319-4917
e-mail: toiawase@hituzi.co.jp
http://www.hituzi.co.jp/
postal transfer 00120-8-142852

ISBN978-4-89476-720-1
Printed in Japan

Acknowledgement and Biography

A story of a remarkable woman's pioneering research
on the phonetics of Japanese and English accents

Shigenobu Sugito

I, Shigenobu Sugito, would like to state my grateful appreciation to many people, who knew Dr. Miyoko Sugito, my mother, and the author of this publication. This publication was embarked upon by many people, after she passed away on the 1st of Feb. in 2012. It was impossible without their great effort of editing for this publication. I would like to give my best regards to the many people who were involved in this publication project.

Let me start to describe my memory of my mom, Miyoko. I still have memories of my mom reading me "Mother Goose Stories" when I was a very small boy before falling asleep. I don't actually have this memory, but rather this story was imprinted on me from mom's telling me. Maybe this was one of the reasons why I hated to learn English before my university time; however, I can understand now it was because I was her mother's boy.

Miyoko and I graduated together in a series of stepping ladders of the school system in Japan, from junior high school to university. This was just a matter of coincidence, of course, but this procedure was a very good actual education for me. I hated her vocational position as a school teacher, but I learned from her an attitude of studying, maybe. However, I chose a different area, cultural anthropology, as a result.

Miyoko was born as the third daughter of Hachiro and Toki Kogure in Tokyo in 1919. Originally, the Hachiro Kogure family had their residence in Ikaho Onsen (hot springs, 伊香保温泉) in Gunma Prefecture (群馬県), which is located in the north of Tokyo. However, Hachiro failed in his business in his hometown and chose to live in Tokyo with his family. Miyoko attended Hongo Elementary School (本郷小学校) at the of age 6 in 1925, not Seishi Elementary School (誠之小学校). Pupils who lived in that area had to attend Seishi Elementary School, but she didn't go there. She didn't understand the reason why, but as a result she used to go to her elementary school across the Hongo Campus of the University of Tokyo (東京大学本郷キャンパス). Miyoko told this story to her children, to my sister Akiko and me. She would sit on a huge branch near Sanshiro Ike (pond, 三四郎池) in the campus. She named it "gikko no ki", because it made a noise when she sat on it and it shook like a swing.

Miyoko attended Oin Girls High School (桜蔭女学校) after graduation of elementary school in 1931 and after that in 1936, she attended the Tokyo Women's Higher Normal School for Women (東京高等女子師範学校, now known as Ochanomizu University, お茶の水大学. Hereafter referred to as Normal School.) as a liberal art course student. During her high school time, she started to learn English as a private lesson from a certain missionary woman. As a result, she passed the examinations at both Tsuda Institute for English Studies (津田英学塾) and Tokyo Women's Higher Normal School. She might have decided to attend Tsuda Institute; however, her family forced her to attend the Normal School (which was considered to be larger and more prestigious). This was a very understandable decision for children in this situation at the time.

It was a disappointment to her, however, since she had enjoyed so much her school life with many friends and teachers. The Women's Normal School had a boarding school system and all students had to live together in the dormitory in their junior grade at least, even if their residence was in Tokyo. This was the reason why she established very good friendships over her life time. For an example, she and her best friend, Ms. Eiko Takiguchi, had decided to visit Hakushu Kitahara (北原白秋), who was a very famous poet at the time, because they were influenced by a Japanese modern poet study lecture one day. Two of them had become fascinated with Hakushu's school of poets. Later Eiko married Shuji Miya (宮柊二), who become an heir for the Tamanokai (多摩の会) of Hakushu School. Miyoko suffered from tuberculous pleurisy during her Normal School era, and she had to take a leave of absence for eight months. When she had to be in the hospital, Eiko visited her hospital room every day, so she kept a very good friendship with Eiko throughout her life. Miyoko remembered another best friend, Ms. Fujiko Hayashi, who was the daughter of a Christian Minister in Hamamatsu. She and Fujiko used to visit the Christian Church sometimes. They shared a common religious sense with each other. Miyoko said that she was almost baptized. After graduation of Normal School, Miyoko became a teacher in Oin Girl's High School from 1941 to 1944. Dr. Kazue Akinaga, a well-known Japanese phonologist, was a school girl who assisted Miyoko.

In March of 1944, Miyoko married Taminobu Sugito, who was a Captain in the Japanese Army, and a teacher in the War School for Army Engineers at the time. They lived in Nakano, east of Tokyo, near the army war school; however, her husband, Taminobu, was assigned as an engineering regiment commander in the Philippines in August of 1944. It was a very short time of honeymoon, but it was almost the final stage of the Pacific War. Taminobu kept fighting with the American Army in a tropical jangle in Luzon Island about a month after the ending of the war on Aug 15, 1945. He had made his decision to surrender with his last 60 some remaining survivors of about 500 soldiers of his regiment, initially. They were sent to a prison camp where they stayed until the end of 1945. He, finally, came back alive to his parent's house in Osaka in January 1946. Miyoko had been living in Osaka with Taminobu's parents and sister after her husband had gone on the campaign.

Her husband had been purged from any official position because of his official career as a professional army officer, and Miyoko had had to start her new career. She, at the beginning, became a boarding master at Shoin Vocational College for Women (樟蔭女子専門学校) in Osaka from May, 1946. This was not a teaching position but she was satisfied because her job was related to an educational institution. Next March, she moved to the position of secretary at the Education Office of the Osaka Military Government, U.S. Occupation of Japan in 1947, as her friends advised her because of her practical English ability. She worked on research of Japanese culture, visited the Osaka Local Assembly for reporting their discussions, and so on. She enjoyed her job very much, but she had to stop work because of tuberculosis in December, 1948, again. She moved to Ikaho Onsen, her parents' hometown, for recovery and she was supported by her own parents' relatives.

I am not sure when Miyoko came back to her family in Osaka, but she had assumed a teacher position in Shoin Junior High School (樟蔭中学校) in June, 1950. Miyoko and Taminobu had their baby boy, Shigenobu, (me) in July, 1951, and their baby girl, Akiko, in January, 1954.

Miyoko was working as a teacher of Japanese literature at a junior high school, but she was also enjoying her role as advisor and/or producer for the drama club in school. She wrote many scenarios for the drama club, and the club got several prizes from the Osaka League of Drama Clubs for Junior High Schools. As you know, she was born in the Tokyo dialect area of Japan, but she lived in the Osaka dialect area with her family. She was forced to experience such dialect differences in school classes, drama club, conversation with her colleagues and neighbors, and so on. As a result, she decided to audit Professor Hisanosuke Izui's (泉井久之助) linguistics class at the University of Kyoto (京都大学) for two years from 1956. Her age was then 40, and after this, she became a visiting scholar for a year to study dialectal differences. This was the great first step for her academic life as a linguist, phonetician, dialectologist, and so on.

I have no idea how to describe her full academic career in this area, but I can summarize her career after she started her academic life. Her first presentation, "Shibata-san to Imada-san (芝田さんと今田さん)", was presented in 1964 at the Society for the Study of Japanese Language. After this, she presented in 1969, "Osaka-Tokyo Accent and Phonetic Dynamics" at the same society. I think those two presentations were her starting point for her academic life. She was also a "National Language (国語)" teacher in high school and she got her lecturer position at Osaka Shoin Women's University (大阪樟蔭女子大学) in 1971 at the age of 51. I remember that she used to say that her career was tracking that of Shigenobu's attending schools. Shigenobu was a junior high school student in 1964, a high school student in 1969, and a university student in 1971.

I can't remember exactly when her concerns had shifted away from linguistics toward phonetics, but she wrote in this book about an important sudden meeting with Dr. Saburo Uemura (植村三朗) at the Institute of Sony (ソニー研究所) which made her become so interested in phonetics.

I have a deficit of memory about her study concerns from the mid 1970's to early 1980's, because my concern was moving toward my own academic track. But I can remember that we would argue about applicable methodology using statistics and computer technology sometimes. Another important argument point was about her retirement from her university life. The timing was 1989. In the mid 1980's, she had started to organize a big project for research, and her affiliation was a key point for this purpose. I advised her to establish a private research institution on her property. I got my job in Sugiyama Jogakuen University (椙山女学園大学), Nagoya, in 1988, and the house, which I lived in, became empty. I advised her that she could utilize it as her home-base institute. In 1989, she opened the Institute for Speech Communication Research (音声言語研究所), just after her retirement from Osaka Shoin Women's University, at the age of 70.

Also, her big project titled "Integrated Studies on Prosodic Features of Current Japanese Language with Application to Spoken Language Education" (日本語音声における韻律的特徴の実態とその教育に関する総合的研究) was funded by a Grant-in-Aid for Scientific Research on Priority Areas (科学研究費補助金・重点領域研究) by the Japanese Government in 1989 until 1993. A database project of dialect collection followed after this in 1994 and from 1995 to 1997, it was compiled as a DAT (Digital Audio Tape) formatted recording collection. During the big project, Miyoko was nominated president of the Phonetic Society of Japan (日本音声学会) from 1992 to 1995.

Of course, she was active in academics after the big project. She hosted academic monthly meetings from 1997 until 2011, edited and published a series of books from Kuroshio Shuppan (くろしお出版), as fruits of the monthly meetings at her institute. These were her favorite meetings. The meetings were stopped from August, 2011, because of the hot summer weather and also for taking care of her husband, Taminobu, who passed away in the end of October. After a 6 months break, Miyoko decided to reactivate the monthly meetings and announced by email they would start on the 18th of February, 2012;

however, her project became an impossible dream. She suddenly passed away at midnight of the 1st of February at the age of 92, because of obstructive jaundice caused by pancreatic cancer. It is difficult to say but maybe she might be happy to escape from long term hospital admission.

I must close this acknowledgement now. Miyoko was admitted to the hospital twice in her youth for TB. She married a professional military officer. She had two sections of life: one before and one after the Pacific War. She was a good teacher and a good scholar. And also, she lived a happy life with many friends in academics, neighbors, schools, and her family.

Thank you very much, all of you who have worked with Miyoko. Please enjoy reading this book.

A small list of people who helped make this book possible. (listed in alphabetic order)

1. Campbell, Nick
2. Erickson, Donna
3. Fujimoto, Masako
4. Inukai, Takashi
5. Kawahara, Shigeto
6. Kitahara, Mafuyu
7. Masuda, Hinako
8. Sadanobu, Toshiyuki
9. Sato, Hirokazu
10. Sugito, Shigenobu

11. Tajima, Keiichi
12. Yoneyama, Kiyoko
13. Zhu, Chunyue

Shigenobu Sugito

Professor, Sugiyama Jogakuen University

Overall comment by the supervisor

Donna Erickson

I think I first met Miyoko Sugito-sensei in the early 90's, shortly after she had retired, and set up her research lab, "The Institute for Speech Communication Research", next to her house. I was a guest researcher at ATR labs in Kyoto-fu then, and her house was a hop, skip and jump away from ATR. However, it was not a simple hop, skip and jump, because of the way the roads were, and unless you knew where you were going, it was easy to get lost, even for taxis!!

I remember many many conversations with Sugito-sensei, at her house, on the train, on the phone, at many different places. Our connecting point at first was the laryngeal strap muscles, and how they were used in producing low F0 (Fundamental Frequency). Both of us had done EMG work on F0 control, Sugito-sensei on the difference between Kansai and Kanto Japanese, and me on Thai tones. So, we were "sisters" in crime, so to speak. "Crime", because at least at the time of Sugito-sensei's research, it was not widely accepted that the laryngeal strap muscles were involved in F0 control. I think now it has been accepted. We had many long, stimulating talks about tone and pitch and the interaction between vowels and F0 control.

Sugito-sensei always had questions, for instance, in a conversation, why do Japanese tend to repeat what the other person had just said? Do you repeat this much in English conversations? Most of her questions never really had simple answers, but were fun to talk about because they led to new questions and new possible answers.

She was also very kind and wise, and helped me both professionally and personally in many ways. One time, I remember I stayed at their house. It was December. I was singing in a church choir for a Christmas concert, and needed to be in Yokohama by mid-morning. Miyoko and her very kind husband, walked me, in the early morning to the nearest train station, (since no busses were running) so I could make it to sing on time. It was about a 20 or 30 minute walk, and very very cold and dark. I have very special memories of that morning as we cheerfully walked and continued discussing all sorts of interesting things.

Miyoko, I thank you for your pioneering spirit, you curiosity, your youth, your energy, your example especially to us women in the field of speech communication. Thank you!

I am happy that we can publish this book in English. It was started several years ago with the help of Hinako Masuda, as a translation of a Japanese book, which came out in publication several months after her death.

Her wishes were to have this book published in English. I am very happy to finally be able to read in English many of the things Miyoko and I had talked about. Hinako did a wonderful job translating. I just helped with polishing up some sentences. I also thank the following young researchers who contributed their time to helping clarify certain points in the text and figures: Masako Fujimoto, Masafuyu Kitahara, Keiichi Tajima, Kiyoko Yoneyama, and Shigeto Kawahara.

Donna Erickson
Adjunct Faculty Sophia University & Kanazawa Medical University

Overall comment by the translator

Hinako Masuda

I was first offered the opportunity of translating this book through Professor Hirokazu Sato (Tokyo University of Foreign Studies) in February 2011. I was grateful, honored, and thrilled to have the opportunity of translating this book.

To my regret, I ended up not being able to meet Dr. Sugito in person. I was planning a visit to her laboratory during spring vacation (around February to March), and then I received the news. We did, however, have many occasions of talking over the phone. We called each other on a regular basis to talk about the book, and also about other things. I had just finished my Ph.D. and began my career as a lecturer and researcher when I was working on this translation project. I started off as a part-time lecturer at a university, and was worried about my future. I told her about my worries, and she told me, in very simple words, that research is not something to be done in a short period of time, and if you give it some time and not be too hard on yourself, things will fall into place. She also said that the most important thing is to continue doing what you enjoy. Her words had given so much strength to the beginning of my career as a young, female researcher.

I enjoyed the process of translating this book. Many people were involved and provided us with insightful advice. Professor Donna Erickson and I had many meetings and e-mail conversations about this book. I appreciate her patience and generosity throughout the process. We worked very hard because we believe that this book will be a great introductory book on Japanese accent to the general readers. It is different from an ordinary textbook in a way that it includes many personal episodes of Dr. Sugito. I hope that many people have a chance to experience the wonderful world of speech communication.

Hinako Masuda
Assistant professor, Waseda University

Comments on Chapter 1

Toshiyuki Sadanobu and Chunyue Zhu

At present, English borrows various words from Japanese, such as "samurai", "tempura", and "karaoke", while Japanese too borrows countless words from English. It is not uncommon for the same word to exist in both English and Japanese. However, these words' pronunciations when functioning as either English or Japanese words give us completely different impressions. What is the cause of this large discrepancy in impressions? Are there no points of intersection between the English and Japanese pronunciations? If so, what are they?

In this book, Prof. Dr. Miyoko Sugito, who led research on spoken language for about half a century, provides clear answers to the above questions based on the results of her own research. Simultaneously in the book Dr. Sugito looks back over her research career, explaining to a wide range of readers the marvel of the uniquely human act of "speaking" and the joy of understanding this act through research.

Regrettably, this is Dr. Sugito's final book, as she passed away in February 2012. However, her scholarship and her warm, kind personality will not be forgotten. While we cannot adequately thank her for all her teachings and kindness, we have, at the invitation of Prof. Dr. Donna Erickson, and with the help of Ms. Hinako Masuda—joined by friends and volunteers from the next generation of scholars—added some modest comments to each chapter in the hopes that they will aid the reader's understanding in some small way.

The first chapter draws the reader in by discussing the mysteriousness of human speech. It explains the physiological basis of speech and how it distinguishes humans from other animals, in addition to introducing the themes addressed in later chapters, such as accent, intonation, vowels, consonants, devocalization, and rhythm. This chapter is particularly easy to understand and requires little explanation, so the above, together with the preceding background information regarding how we came to write the comments for this book, will conclude our commentary for the first chapter. As we are people who benefited from Dr. Sugito's enthusiastic teaching and warm encouragement, we are extremely happy and proud to have our names added here.

Toshiyuki Sadanobu
Professor, University of Kobe

Chunyue Zhu
Professor, University of Kobe

Comments on Chapter 4

Takashi Inukai

The first half of this chapter explains about the relationship between regional differences in Japanese accent and its historical changes. I will describe the hidden message behind this in hope that readers unfamiliar to the Japanese history will be able to follow the chapter.

The explanation begins with the story of Ikkyu. Ikkyu (1394–1481) is a distinguished priest in the Middle Ages. He was well-known for his sophistication and eccentricity. Later, a book of episodes "Ikkyu shokoku banashi" was written in which Ikkyu, the main character in the episodes, finds his way out of numerous troubles using his great knowledge. The story introduced in this book is the most famous one. The wit of this story is that "hashi" (bridge) and "hashi" (edge) are written in identical *kana* characters. The author of this story begins by informing the readers that the accent types are different, not only between words but also in Tokyo and Kyoto dialects.

In the book "Ruijyumyogisho" published in the first half of the

12th century, a symbol is used to show the syllable tone along with its Japanese reading. The vast number of words in the book makes clear the Kyoto accent at that time.

Japanese accent research has an important concept of "lexical classification". Words are classified according to their accent types, and they are identical across dialects. For example, a word that is classified as Group 1 in the Tokyo List will also be classified as Group 1 in the Kyoto List. Its chronological changes will be recorded within the group. The dialect spoken in Kyoto and Osaka is called Kansai type dialect, which is considered as the central in Japanese dialect. Dialect spoken east and west of Kansai type dialect is called Tokyo type dialect. Dialect spoken east and west of Tokyo type dialect is called no accent or Type II accent. Japanese researchers believe that, in this way, dialectal accent propagated throughout the country from Kansai area which used to be the heart of politics in ancient times. It is said that the modern accent system where accent varies according to regions was established during Edo era (1603~1867).

To explain this accent propagation, the author introduces Murasakishikibu, a noble female who wrote the story of Genjimonogatari. This story took ten years to complete, and its writing process took place around the year 1000. Murasakishikibu probably had a Kyoto accent. Those who lived around the time of revolutionary era between Edo and Meiji would have spoken in various accents according to regions. Japan's feudal government called Bakufu was located in Edo (Tokyo as of now) with the chief called Shogun. The last Shogun, Yoshinobu Tokugawa, probably spoke with an Edo dialect. The court nobles probably spoke with a Kyoto dialect. Political forces fighting against Edo Bakufu were the Choshu Domain in Yamaguchi prefecture, Satsuma Domain in Kagoshima prefecture, and Tosa Domain in Kochi prefecture. Ryoma Sakamoto was from Tosa, and Takamori Saigo and Toshimichi Okubo were from Satsuma. They obtained key positions after their victory of the Boshin Civil War. They formed cliques, for example Choshu clique for the army and Satsuma clique for the navy. The author suggests that regional dialects strengthened their bonds and developed their incentives.

The author also refers to Kansai accent as the original Japanese accent, and that the regional accents in Japan spread from Kansai area. She referred to this idea in our personal conversation before she passed away. There is a region in the mountainous area in southern Nara (northern part of Wakayama prefecture, southern to Totsugawa village) where its dialect is similar to that of Tokyo. Jinmu, the first Japanese Emperor, disembarked in Kii (Wakayama as of now), pursued north, and was enthroned in Yamato, the center of Nara prefecture. The author wonders about the relationship between this historical incident and accent prototype. Lewis Ramsey suspects that the accent in current Kansai dialect takes a new form according to the principle of accent propagation, and reformed the accent system similar to that of modern Tokyo, with reference to Ruijyumyogisho. The discussion continues even now. What did the author think of this? Unfortunately, we cannot find that out.

The following chapters will describe the procedure of how to interpret accent by looking at recorded sound waves, and that the

English accent is affected by pitch. I will leave the readers to decode them.

Takashi Inukai
Professor, Aichi Prefectural University

FOREWORD

This book introduces as well as answers many questions about the word accent of Japanese and English.

It has long been said that Japanese has a pitch accent and that English has a stress accent. But if someone asks me, "So… how are they different?" it is very difficult for me to explain. In order to look further into it, I began to experiment by a machine that changes the sound, given from the SONY research laboratory, into sound waves. This was more than 50 years ago, in the days when there were no computers. I closely surveyed the change in the pitch and stress within hundreds of sound waves in Japanese (Tokyo and Kansai, in particular) and English.

I then found out that there were unexpected similarities between Japanese and English accents (or between Kansai and English accents, to be exact). In order to solve this mystery, I tried to conduct as many experiments as I could possibly come up with. And this is how the long journey began.

In those years, I was able to conduct many experiments with the

Acoustics and Phonetics Laboratory in the Department of Engineering, and the Phonetics Laboratory (Research Institute of Logopedics and Phoniatrics) at the University of Tokyo. I will clarify the issues by also using the results obtained from those experiments.

Next, I would like to ask the readers whether they knew that the usage of word accent in sentences or conversations is completely different for English and Japanese native speakers. In this book, I would also like to explain the differences in the usage of the two speaker groups based on the results obtained from various experiments, and also to comment on a strategy for the pronunciation of a Japanese speaker of English to become closer to that of a native speaker of English.

INTRODUCTION:
"Sound waves" from SONY

Life is full of unexpected events, and they may take over your life. —— I think I was on my way home from a conference held in Tokyo when I visited the SONY laboratory for the first time. This happened almost 50 years ago.

I decided to go for a visit because I found out in the newspaper that the newlywed Crown Prince (the Emperor as of now!) and Crown Princess had paid a visit to SONY. Back in those days, there was no synthesized speech that could be clearly understood. However, the newspaper article said that SONY had welcomed them with "Thank you for visiting, Crown Prince" in synthesized Japanese speech.

The newspaper said that SONY tried to develop highly comprehensible synthesized speech by doing the following: —— "The sound recorded onto a tape is played at the speed of 1/100 and transformed into sound waves by using a machine called 'oscilocoda'. Then the sound waves are handwritten onto a long paper, traced with a pen, and transformed into electrical pressure. —— The sound is played at a thousand times speed. —— Synthesized speech made in such a way had high intelligibility."

At that time, there was an established theory that the principle of

Japanese accent cannot be known by experiments. But I wanted to know whether it really was so.

Right around that time, I (Tokyo-born) called on "Imada-san" in a classroom, but "Shibata-san" came up instead. The two names are completely different in Chinese characters, but when I wrote the two names 'Imada, Shibata' in alphabet on the palm of my hand, I realized that the accent was the same, and the vowel sounds were the same. This is how I came to look up all the three-kana last names (348 households) from the Osaka telephone directory (not as thick as the Tokyo one), and to examine the Tokyo and Osaka accents.

In Tokyo, the high accent is on 'SHI' in 'SHIbata-san' and 'I' in 'Imada-san' (or 'iMADA san'), (thus, but these names have the same accent pattern), but in Osaka, high accent is on 'SAN' in 'Shibata SAN' and 'MA' in 'IMAda san'. In this case, —— of the Osaka dialect, the differences are apparent. Accent varies a great deal according to dialects. However, there are common rules among them, and I came to realize that the rules may have something to do with the combination of sounds. It all happened around that time...

Well, there was nobody at the entrance of SONY Laboratory. But luckily, a researcher-looking man with a white gown was walking past a nearby hall, and he came over to me and said "Is there anything I can help you with?" I told him what I had come to the laboratory for, and he kindly showed me around. He was, by chance, Dr. Saburo Uemura, the developer of 'oscilocoda'.

He showed me the oscilocoda, and I listened to the synthesized speech and his explanations. After some time, he began to ask me some questions. Why did I want to listen to the speech sound? Why did I want to see the machine? What are my research interests? As I answered his questions, I assumed that my true intention, that is, to investigate the principle of accent, might not be understood.

However, just as I was about to leave, he said, "What do you want to convert to sound waves? Please record the sound and send it to us. We can convert it to sound waves by using osilocoda, and send it back to you like a scroll". I was surprised at his generosity, thanked him, and went home. Everything that happened was a coincidence. But in reality, I had no recorder, microphone, or recording tapes. It may be hard to imagine, but that was the time when Japan was going through postwar reconstruction period.

—— "Densuke" recorder for broadcasting stations

A recorder called "Densuke" for broadcasting stations, arrived a few days later (the name of which I found out later) along with a high-priced microphone and recording tapes, which might have been sample products. These were what the NHK interviewers used for recordings on the streets with the microphone towards the speaker. It was an open-reel, high-quality recorder whose tapes could be seen from the outside as well.

I used "Densuke" to record words and short sentences spoken in the Osaka accent I was interested in, and sent them to the SONY Laboratory. This is how rolls and rolls of long paper with sound wave transcriptions began to arrive.

I am from Tokyo, which perhaps made me proud about my "standard accent". When I moved to Osaka, what I got was "You have a really heavy accent! I can't understand you!" and this was shocking to me. But this incident is what made me discover my precious interest. There were accents such as "aMEe (rain)", "aSAa (morning)", "aKIi (autumn)", "haRUu (spring)", and "aHOo (idiot)", and they begged me to pay attention to them.

—— Working without a manual

The piece of paper that records sound waves only has continuous jaggy waves. But the work of writing down the words as I listened to the sound and observed the sound waves was actually rather amusing. I gradually became accustomed to it, and was able to guess the Osaka accent of the word by just looking at the waves. Next, I measured the amplitude of the vowels, the durations of vowels and consonants, and also the fundamental frequency. Questions arose one after another. Normally, the pitch in the steady state (the most stable part) of the vowel is what determines the value of Hertz. However, when I measured, I found out it wasn't that simple. The fact was that the pitch changes over time gave rise to many questions, and I ended up measuring the cycle of sound waves with utmost detail —— that is, measuring every single wavelength (later changing it to Hertz by calculating the inverse of them). A bookworm that used to shed tears reading the original text of Tales of Genji, was trying to extract pitch, in her own style. —— Yes, there are unexpectedly fun things in life even when you are ever so busy.

Yes. It was like going on an adventure to a place where no one has ever set foot before. Many questions arose as I measured the high-low changes in the voice. Among those were questions regarding the "delayed descent" and "there is an accent in unvoiced mora" which I will explain in later chapters.

—— "Pen-oscillo", a machine that draws sound waves, is here!

The "pen-oscillo" arrived unexpectedly. I was very surprised. The appearance of this machine was unappealing, as if someone had put together some old machinery parts. However, it was like a treasure to me. This simple, special machine punched out, on one particular spot, one meter of sound waves onto a recording paper for every one second of sound. As silly as it sounds, my husband was the one who signed his name on the receipt when these items were delivered to our house. Maybe women those days had no rights to do so?

When the machine was having troubles, Mr. Himuro, an engineer, kindly came all the way to West Osaka (where we used to live at that time) on a night train that arrived early Sunday morning, took a day to fix it after breakfast, and went back to Tokyo that very night on the night train.

There were so many people who kindly supported me, although I had not even met them before. This is how I was blessed with the great experiment environment that could not be seen anywhere else. In the very beginning, it was just a visit out of curiosity, and look how it has now turned out.

—— Encounter and fate is magic. ——

Recordings again: the basics of word accent

I started using the "pen-oscillo", and I came up with the idea of collecting Tokyo and Osaka accent data. I wanted to be able to explain everything!

In order to do so, I made a list of 556 words that consisted of one mora (for example, "e" [picture] and "o" [tail]) to six mora (for example, "i-ro-e-n-pi-tsu" [colored pencil]). I made a list of the words (later randomly), and decided to record the sounds as uttered by pure Tokyo and Osaka speakers. The speakers were Mr. Teranishi (originally from the old city of Tokyo) who worked for SONY in Osaka, and Mr. Araki (a young master at a traditional store that sells gifts in Semba, the center of Osaka).

The speech sounds were transformed into sound waves by the "pen-oscillo" one after another. From the pen-oscillo output, I read the vowels and consonants, measured the amplitude and duration of the sound waves, and extracted the fundamental frequency from each wavelength. It was a big challenge that took several years.

What's more, the work we now do to "synthesize" speech, involves simply using the computer to cut pieces of sounds and join them together. I tried out many ways to synthesize speech by hand and splicing and connecting recorded tapes by using the open-reel Densuke. It was the beginning of mystery-solving, and a valuable experience for my later research.

I felt that I had begun to understand about the function of human language more than anyone, after years of dedication and observation. And not only was it a lot of fun, it had become my life work. To me, research is about both fun and work, and I enjoy it. It all started when I decided to visit the SONY laboratory. You never know what will change your life.

Well, let us now look into the world of accent. I think you can say that this is an encounter if you begin to see the world in a different way as you read through the chapters. If so, I will be ever so delighted and thankful.

Contents

Acknowledgement and Biography	i
Overall comment by the supervisor	xi
Overall comment by the translator	xiv
Comments on Chapter 1	xvi
Comments on Chapter 4	xviii
FOREWORD	xxiii
INTRODUCTION: "Sound waves" from SONY	xxv

CHAPTER 1: What does it mean to 'speak'?   1

1–1	What is 'accent'?	1
1–2	How do human beings speak?	3
1–3	How human beings came to speak	6
1–4	How are vowels and consonants made?	8

CHAPTER 2: Rhythm of Japanese and English   11

2–1	Rhythm of Japanese	11
2–2	Rhythm of English	15

CHAPTER 3: "Sound" and "voice" in Japanese and English   19

3–1	Mobile phones and the Japanese syllabary	19
3–2	The value of the Japanese syllabary	21
3–3	The system of Japanese syllabary	23
3–4	Japanese accent and its symbols	24
3–5	English sounds and the alphabet	26
3–6	Features of English accent and its symbols	27

CHAPTER 4: History of accent and the traditional way of thinking   29

4–1	Dialectal accent in Japanese and its history	29
4–2	Observing sound waves	37
4–3	How accent was apprehended	40
4–4	Difference between "hanakago (flower basket)" and "hana kago (flower and basket)"	44
4–5	Brief history of English accent	46

CHAPTER 5: "Late fall" and "accent on voiceless mora"   49

5–1	"Japanese has a pitch accent" —— is this really true?	49
5–2	What is "late fall"? —— Is intensity a factor?	51
5–3	What does "accent on a voiceless mora" mean?	53
5–4	The cause of "late fall"	55
5–5	What is an accent with a falling pitch?	56
5–6	The unexpected discovery!	60

CHAPTER 6: How do English native speakers perceive Japanese accent?   65

6–1	Experiment on how English native speakers perceive Japanese accent	65
6–2	Features of English accent	68
6–3	The nature of Japanese and English accents	69
6–4	Duration and pitch of syllables	71
6–5	How would you interpret English accent?	74

CHAPTER 7: Perception of accent: it is determined by pitch, not intensity!   77

7–1	Discovering the mystery of "late fall" —— its synthesized sounds	78
7–2	40 synthesized "ame" based on an accent production model	83

7–3	pérmit – permít as produced by the accent production model	87
7–4	Perceptual experiment with no-accent type speakers in six cities	90

CHAPTER 8: Accent commands from the brain —— electromyography 95

8–1	What is electromyography?	95
8–2	Muscle activity features recorded from electromyography when speaking with Kansai dialect	99
8–3	How about 'electromyography' when speaking in English?	100
8–4	EMG productions of [a] and [i] are different	104
8–5	The reason I wanted English 'electromyography'	106

CHAPTER 9: Observing the 'accent command' from the brain 109

9–1	Combination of 'mora sound' and 'voice pitch'	109
9–2	The answer to the puzzle —— matching the timing of 'sound of the mora' to the 'voice pitch'	112
9–3	I got it! —— Both Japanese and English have pitch accents!	115

CHAPTER 10: What is the difference between English and Japanese accent? 117

10–1	English and Japanese accent, and the characteristics of narration	117
10–2	Comparison of Japanese and English narrations	119
10–3	Which words are emphasized?	121
10–4	Which parts should have a high pitch?	124
10–5	Variations of 'two bags' by 18 English and Japanese speakers	127
10–6	'Momotaro' by Japanese and English speakers —— What are the differences?	128
10–7	Intonation pattern of the reading	130

10–8	Fundamental differences of English and Japanese speakers' 'English accent'	131
10–9	Application to English pronunciation teaching	134

Epilogue 137

Reference 141

INDEX 149

Column 1:	What is "vowel devoicing"?	10
Column 2:	Example of an accented devoiced mora	17
Column 3:	Accent in the people in dramas —— Kansai accent and Heian era accent	36
Column 4:	Accent of Totsukawamura	40
Column 5:	Accent and intonation	44
Column 6:	Accent of "sankakkei (triangle)"	54
Column 7:	Kansai accent of "**A**me (rain)" with a falling pitch	62
Column 8:	A gift from a child with golden hair	75

CHAPTER 1:

What does it mean to 'speak'?

> Spoken speech is by far the most convenient and efficient way for people to communicate. If you compare spoken speech with singing, both consist of lyrics (sounds of the words) and the melody (voice pitch). Speech is like the combination of songwriting and composing.
>
> The sounds of speech simply use the process of breathing, which is the exhalation that we breathe in to live, and the inhalation that we use to eat (tongue, teeth, alveolar ridge, jaw, etc. See Figure 1–4.). In doing so, you are using the combination of "sound" and "voice pitch". For example, when you say "Ame!", "A" is high-pitched, and the next "me" is low-pitched. High-low or low-high pitches in words are fixed according to dialect. This is what we call accent.

1–1 What is 'accent'?

We use exhalation for producing **voice**. The exit of which the exhalation from the lungs comes out is in the **throat**. Put your fingers on your throat (about where your Adam's Apple is), and make a sound. The **vocal folds** inside your throat vibrate. However, if you simply open your mouth and exhale, you will see there is no sound, and the air is simply going out from your mouth. Try humming with your mouth closed. If you try to say "mu mu mu", or "nn, n, n" with your mouth slightly open, you will be able to feel your breath coming out of your nose. If you place your fingers on your throat, you will be able to feel the vibration of your vocal folds. This is a phenomenon associated with producing voice. Melody is made by voice pitch. Accents of words are made by voice pitch as well.

"**A**me" as in "rain", and "a**ME**" as in "candy". How do you distinguish these two words? "**A**me" and "a**ME**" have the same sounds, but they are different words that have different meanings. The statement, "You distinguish them by the Chinese characters", is true only when you are talking about the writing. So how do we distinguish them when we say or hear them?

When you say "**A**me" (rain), you control the pitch by producing "A" with a high pitch, and "me" with a low pitch. Similarly in the case of "a**ME**" (candy), you produce "a" with a low pitch, and "Me" with a high pitch. In this way, we combine "sound" and "voice pitch" when we speak. Each word has its own set of combinations of "high-low" or "low-high" pitches. In the cases of "ha**NA**" (flower) and "ha**NA**" (nose), when you add the nominative particle 'ga', you can tell the difference between the two words ("ha**NA**-ga" (flower) and "ha**NA**-**GA**" (nose)). This illustrates how we distinguish words —— by using pitch.

We listen to each sound in this way, and we are able to distinguish meanings by listening to the differences in the pitch only. This is called the "accent" of a word.

For example, as early as when a baby begins to learn the word "mama", the pitch of the sound is also learned together with the word. That is, the two movements (producing sound and producing accent in order to give variety to pitch) work together simultaneously. Moreover, we are talking by producing series of words continuously.

Accent varies among dialects. The Kansai accent in Kyoto, Nara, and Osaka, which used to be the standard dialect area, and the Tokyo accent in the Edo area, are so different that they appear to sound just the opposite. This will cause confusion. There used to be an argument about whether to make the dialect of the hometown (Kyoto) of the Meiji emperor the standard dialect, or the dialect of the place where the Emperor resided (Tokyo). In the end, the language spoken by the well-educated people of Tokyo became the standard. Dialects around the nation, including the Kansai dialect, are going through changes; however, there are areas where dialects are still intact.

1-2   How do human beings speak?

Accent is set for each word, and its acquisition begins from infancy. Infants sometimes can be heard to restate words when they make mistakes in accents. It suggests that the accent becomes

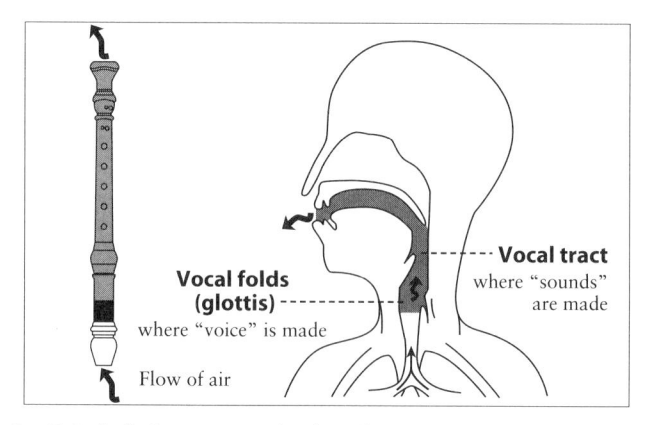

Figure 1-1 Exhaled air creates voice by vibrating the vocal folds in the larynx

entrenched in the brain in a specific form, and it tends to remain unchanged throughout life.

Intonation, on the other hand, changes in each utterance. It changes according to emotion, intention, and differences in the nuance. Listeners often understand the speakers' message through intonation. There are many languages that have a rising pitch at the end of an utterance when asking questions. Such changes in the pitch of the voice are called intonation.

We make **sounds** by using the organs we use for eating. The main players are the jaw, and the tongue that rests on it. When exhalation passes through the vocal tract (the path of voice, from the throat to lips), the jaw moves, and the tongue and lips change shapes simultaneously. Meanings will be conveyed when you say "ai (love)", "ao (blue)", "ie (house)", "ue (up)", etc.

Japanese "a, i, u, e, o" are called **vowels**. Exhalation vibrates the vocal folds, and the air goes out from the lips without any blockage.

CHAPTER 1: What does it mean to 'speak'? 5

Figure 1–2 shows the MRI images (often used at hospitals) inside the oral cavity when pronouncing "a, i, u, e, o". The tongue positions are different for each vowel. Please pronounce the vowels and try to intuit how the tongue shape changes in your mouth, and compare its

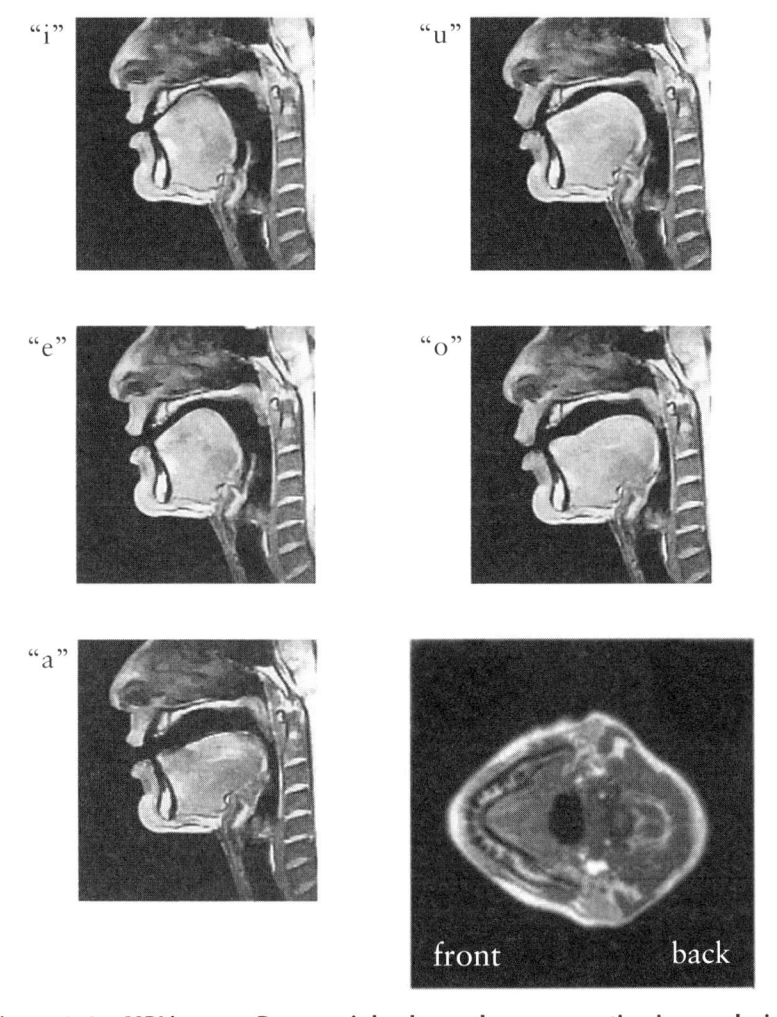

Figure 1–2   MRI images. Bottom right shows the cross-section image during articulation

movement with Figure 1–2.

The bottom part of Figure 1–2 shows the cross-sectional view. If you observe the movements of the mouth closely, you can see that each part is moving a lot while the participant speaks. It is thrilling to think that these sensitive and complex movements are being carried out unconsciously!

Only moving your mouth does not produce vowels. Sounds are produced when voice is made with the vibration of the vocal folds, as well as sounds made by changing the shape of the oral cavity. It only works when these two movements are made at a proper timing.

Please do try them out, as you would understand it more deeply if you open your mouth and make sounds yourself.

The ascent and descent of voice pitch by accent has a lot to do with pronunciation. Chapters 8 and 9 will explain, by looking into specific muscle movement commands from the brain, how Japanese speak Japanese, and English speakers speak English. I would like you to understand in detail what it is to 'speak'. It is spectacular.

1–3   How human beings came to speak

Dogs and cats are able to make sounds, but they cannot speak. Human beings are the only species that are able to speak. Animals can convey messages through making sounds, but they are not able to communicate complicated contents by using complex grammar.

Come to think of it, we combine sounds at great speed to create

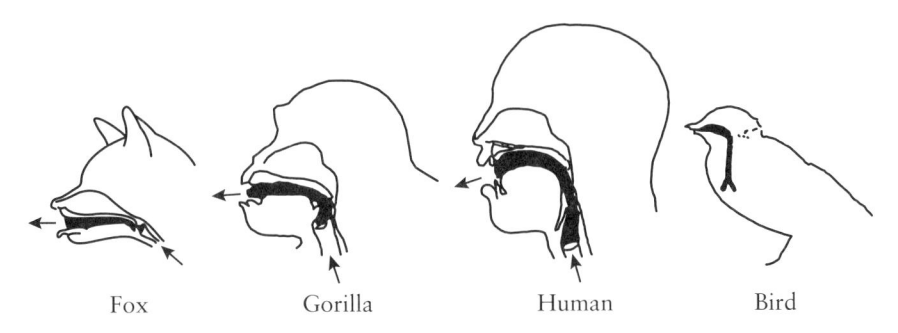

Figure 1-3 Vocal tracts of fox, primate, human and bird

words beyond what are in the dictionary. With accent and intonation included! Although individuals vary, some people are able to produce sentences with six to seven letters in one second. And to top it off, we can even change the sound and the voice pitch in the middle of the procedure.

Parrots and myna birds that have long vocal tracts are able to produce words like "Ohayo, ojosan (good morning, young lady)". However, they are not able to change the expression even if the person is a male. They are just copying the sounds. It is fundamentally different from human beings "speaking".

It is thought that human beings being able to speak have something to do with their being able to walk on two feet. After many generations of being able to walk on two feet, the vocal tract became longer (see Figure 1-3). Longer vocal tracts are able to make more complex sounds. It is impossible to produce various sounds that are necessary to make speech with vocal organs of dogs and cats.

I hear that there are dolphins that are able to communicate with human beings. Dolphins and whales, and elephant herds communicate by low-frequency sounds. It will be quite exciting if we are able to chat with dolphins and whales, but it will take a long time for that to come true, if ever.

1–4　How are vowels and consonants made?

Sounds are distinguished by blocking the exhaled air by closing our lips, and touching the lips, alveolar ridge, and palate (see Figure 1–4) with our tongue or teeth. The palate consists of the **hard palate** and **soft palate** (**velum**). If you trace the roof of your mouth with your fingers, you can feel that the front part is hard. That is the hard palate. If you move your fingers towards the back, it feels icky and you will no longer be able to touch that part. That part is quite soft compared to the hard palate —— therefore, it is called the soft palate.

Let's take a look at the relation between pronunciation and vocal organs.

(1) Close your lips before you produce "a". The air comes out from your nose, and the sound becomes [ma].
(2) Place your tongue behind your top front teeth, and say "a" as you tap there. The sound is [ta].
(3) Place your tongue behind your upper teeth, exhale from your nose, and open your mouth. The sound is [na].

CHAPTER 1: What does it mean to 'speak'? 9

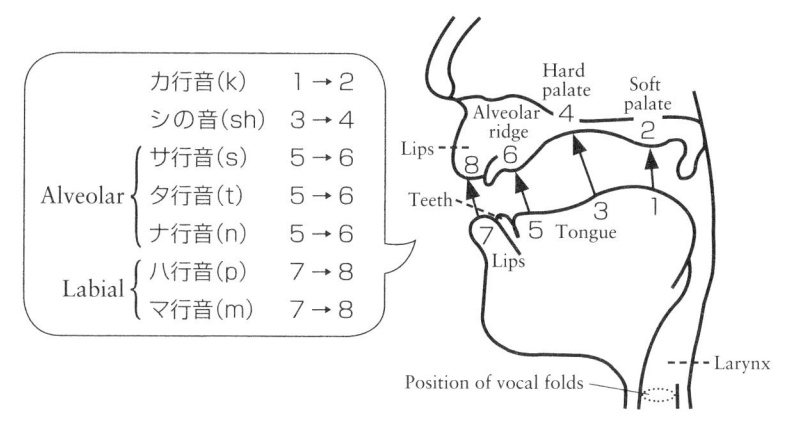

```
           カ行音 (k)    1 → 2
           シの音 (sh)   3 → 4
         ┌ サ行音 (s)    5 → 6
Alveolar ┤ タ行音 (t)    5 → 6
         └ ナ行音 (n)    5 → 6
         ┌ ハ行音 (p)    7 → 8
Labial   ┤
         └ マ行音 (m)    7 → 8
```

Figure 1–4 Emergence of "voice" and individual "sounds"

The [t m n] consonants are made like this. Please try it out yourself.

(4) Place your tongue flat against the lower jaw. Narrow the space between your tongue and the roof of your mouth, and exhale. The friction of the air makes the sound [s]. If you vibrate your vocal folds, it becomes [z].

Please be aware of the following three points in the system of vocalization:

(a) Is the air coming out from your mouth or your nose?
(b) Tongue position
(c) How you produce the sound

The air is not blocked when you produce vowels. Consonants [m n] are called **nasals,** because the lips or the teeth block the air and make it go out through the nose. In the case of [t], air is blocked for a moment by raising the tongue. The back of the tongue is raised in [k], and also blocks the air. Place your fingers in your mouth and say "ka-ka-ka", and compare with [t]. [t k] are sounds made by plosion, so they are called **plosives.** [s] is called a **fricative** because there is a frication sound. The tongue plays a big part in making sounds. These sounds, in which the air is blocked partially or completely by the lips or tongue are called **consonants.**

Also, consonants may be divided into two groups: **voiced consonants** (such as [m n g d]) that involve the vibration of the vocal folds, and **voiceless consonants** (such as [s t p k]) that are produced with no vibration.

> **Column 1: What is "vowel devoicing"?**
>
> In Japanese, the word "strike (su-to-ra-i-ku)" can be counted as five units. In other words, a mora is a set made up of one consonant and one vowel. Speakers other than the Kansai dialect (although there is a tendency of Kansai dialect speakers recently as well) devoice the vowel in the first and fifth mora as in the example of [s-toraik-]. That is, vowels [u ɪ] are often devoiced when voiceless consonants such as [s t] are adjacent. For example, /u/ between voiceless consonants /s/ and /t/ (/u/ in /su/), and vowels after a voiceless consonant /k/ (/u̥/ in /ku̥/) are omitted; so only the consonant is pronounced. In such cases, vocal folds do not vibrate, and there is no voice. Thus, it is called vowel devoicing.
>
> However, we usually do not recognize that we are omitting vowels. "What happened to the vowel?" We "think" we are pronouncing the vowel. We count it as one mora even if there is no actual sound. Such an interesting phenomenon!

CHAPTER 2:

Rhythm of Japanese and English

> When we sing, dance, as well as listen and watch, we tend to use our hands and feet as we feel the rhythm. How about the case of rhythm with regard to spoken language? How do Japanese and English speakers deal with it?
>
> The characteristics of such rhythm are what makes Japanese and English the languages they are. Let's look at how they work.

2-1　Rhythm of Japanese

Japanese uses several writing systems such as kana, Chinese characters, and Roman alphabet.

The following poem "Hananonononohana" is by Shuntaro Tanigawa, one of the poets that represent Japan.

The example in (1) is written in kana letters, which the original text was written in. The example in (2) is a mixture of Chinese characters and kana, and (3) is written in Roman alphabet.

Please try reading them aloud.

(1) In kana form
　　はなののののはな (hananonononohana)
　　はなのななあに (hananonanaani)
　　なずななのはな (nazunananohana)
　　なもないのばな (namonainobana)

(2) In kana and Chinese characters
　　花野の野の花 (hananonononohana)
　　花の名なあに (hananonanaani)
　　なずな菜の花 (nazunananohana)
　　名もない野花 (namonainobana)

(3) In alphabetical letters
　　hananonononohana
　　hananonanaani
　　nazunananohana
　　namonainobana

Translation:
Wild flowers in the garden
What is the name of this flower?
Is it shepherd's purse or field mustard?
Wild flowers with no name.

　　(1) is rather difficult to read, because of the continuous stream of kana. (2) is quite easy to read for speakers of Japanese, because it is a

CHAPTER 2: Rhythm of Japanese and English

mixture of kana and Chinese characters. Even so, Tanigawa uses only kana, sacrificing ease of reading. This is probably because he wants the rhythm of the language to take priority in the rhythm of the language. over reading ease.

(3) is separated into vowels and consonants. They are broken down into small units so that we are able to see what is inside each sound. There are consonants in front of each of the vowels, such as "a, o, i, u, e". You can see that most kana consists of "one vowel" or "a set of consonant and vowel". Each kana is a mora that constitutes the Japanese rhythm.

Let's look at Figure 2–1. This figure shows the durations of each consonant and vowel in the recordings of poems. Try reading it aloud and feel the rhythm by tapping on something. (■ indicates a mora-length pause)

h	a	n	a	n	o	n	o	n	o	n	o	h	a	n	a
は		な		の		の		の		の		は		な	

h	a	n	a	n	o	n	a	n		a	a	n	i		
は		な		の		な		な		あ		に			

	n	a	z	u	n	a	n	a	n	o	h	a	n	a	
	な		ず		な		な		の		は		な		

n	a	m	o	n	a	i		n	o	b	a	n	a		
な		も		な		い		の		ば		な			

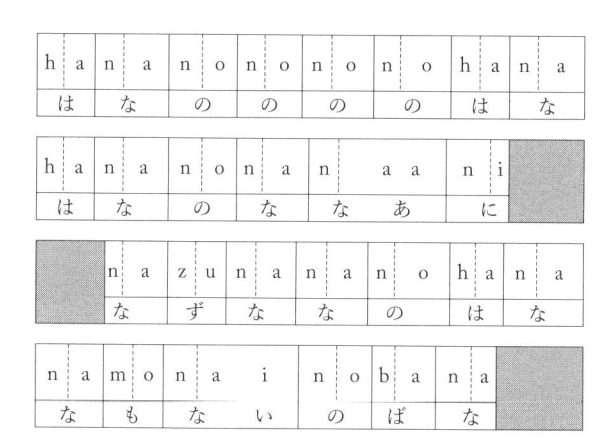

Figure 2-1 Measurement of consonant and vowel duration

I measured the durations of consonants and vowels. The durations of each sound for each line of poetry, including the pauses, fits perfectly inside a square (Figure 2–1). In this case, we are able to count the inserted pause as one mora, just as we are able to count "one vowel" or "a set of consonant and vowel" as one mora.

The following poems are also excerpts from Tanigawa's work:

(4) かっぱかっぱらった (kappakapparatta)
　　かっぱらっぱかっぱらった (kapparattakapparatta)
　　とってちってた (tottechitteta)

Translation:
Kappa (Japanese monster) stole.
Kappa stole a trumpet,
and ran far away.

(5) やんまにがした (yanmanigashita)
　　ぐんまのとんま (gunmanotonma)
　　さんまをやいて (sanmawoyaite)
　　あんまとたべた (anmatotabeta)

Translation:
I let the dragonfly fly away.
A dummy in Gunma (place in Japan).
Cooked a brevoot (kind of fish).
Ate it with a massage practioner.

We can see two types of exceptions here.

/Q/ is called a geminate (shown as two letters, e.g. "pp" in "kappa"), and /N/ is called a Japanese syllabic nasal (shown as "n"). /Q/ is actually only a pause. The lengthening (represented here by an additional vowel) of the two morae word "na ni" to a three morae "na a ni" is also counted as one mora. The lengthening holds the same duration as "one vowel" or "a set of consonant and vowel"; therefore, the lengthening is counted as one mora. In Japanese, the duration of a sound that may be expressed by one kana is considered as one mora, and it is this which makes the rhythm of Japanese language.

The mora is fundamental to many of the Japanese haiku and poems, in which five and seven morae are used. Such rhythm is also used in prose, some of them as old as stories such as "Tales of Heike" and works by Kenji Miyazawa.

The rhythm of Japanese is made by adjusting the word duration into a set number of morae.

2–2 Rhythm of English

You can see that imported words such as "su-to-ra-i-ku (strike)" and "su-to-re-e-to (straight)" have five morae. In other words, these are five morae words. "bo-o-ru (ball)" is a three morae word, and "ni-n-gyo-o (doll)" is a four morae word.

What is the difference in accent between Japanese "sutoraiku" and English "strike"? Here, we are only talking about the Tokyo accent. Accented morae are underlined.

The English words 'strike, straight' have a set of vowels "i" (pronounced as [aɪ]) and "ai" (pronounced as [eɪ]), have accents, and have some consonants surrounding them. It is fundamentally different from the simple structure of "one vowel" or "consonant + vowel" as seen with Japanese. In English, successive vowels are considered as one unit. Successive English vowels such as [aɪ] are not made of [a] and [ɪ], but rather one vowel [aɪ]. Therefore, in this respect, Japanese and English hold a different perspective on how to treat vowels.

Rhythm may be thought of as repetitions of sounds with similar durations. This is the same for Japanese and English, but the way of putting sounds together is different. In Japanese, words become longer when the number of kana increases. In English, on the other hand, words do not necessarily become longer with increased number of letters, and you can control the duration by pronouncing the word partially faster.

Let's try saying the following words with English rhythm. (1), (2) and (3) are all different in terms of word length, but they can be pronounced in the same duration.

(1) One, two, three, four.
(2) One and, two and, three and, four.
(3) One of the teachers is coming to tea.

(1)	One,	two,	three,	four.
(2)	One and,	two and,	three and,	four.
(3)	One of the	teachers is,	coming to	tea.

The durations of '(1) One', '(2) One and', and '(3) One of the' are approximately the same (duration of phonation). Similarly, the durations of '(1) two', '(2) two and', and '(3) teacher is', as well as '(1) three', '(2) three and', and '(3) coming to' are approximately the same.

In this way, a speaker may partially change the speed in order to adjust the phonation duration. In Japanese, the rhythm may be adjusted with the number of letters, and not change the duration of morae. In English, on the other hand, the rhythm may be adjusted by changing the duration of words (changing the speed of certain words).

Figure 2–2 illustrates the differences between "sutoraiku" in Japanese and "strike" in English.

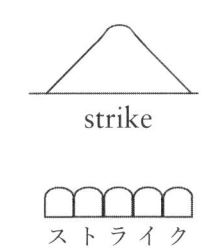

Figure 2–2　Japanese "sutoraiku" and English "strike"

> **Column 2:　Example of an accented devoiced mora**
>
> Both "strike" and "straight" are one-syllable English words. For example, the first vowel is devoiced and the accent is on the second mora for the Japanese words "ku̥sa (grass)", "ku̥se (habit)", and "ki̥ta (north)" in a Tokyo accent. However, in Kansai, the accent in the words "ku̥sa (grass)", "ku̥se (habit)", "ki̥ta (north)", "shi̥ka (deer)", and "fu̥sa (bunch)" is on the first mora. Let's try pronouncing them. There are cases in the young generation that the accent is on the devoiced mora. Why is it so? We shall unveil the mystery in Chapter 5.

CHAPTER 3:

"Sound" and "voice" in Japanese and English

> Words consist of "vowels" and "consonants". There are roughly five vowels in Japanese, produced in similar durations, they may be preceded by a consonant. Each Vowel or Consonant plus Vowel is called a "mora". Each word is made from one mora or a combination of several morae.
>
> In English, on the other hand, one or several consonants are adjacent to a vowel or a diphthong, and form a "syllable". In this case, the accent is on one vowel (or a diphthong). There are many cases where more than two consonants are present.

3-1 Mobile phones and the Japanese syllabary

If you ask a child whether the sound of one *kana* can be broken down into two or more, the answers will more or less be like this:

"ka, sa, ta, na, ha" are just like "a, i, u, e, o". You can't break them up.

It is true that [a] cannot be broken down into a smaller unit, but

[ka], [sa], [ta], and [na] consist of a consonant and a vowel, so they can be broken down into consonants and vowels. We just do not consciously think that they consist of two units.

When we use mobile phones, the first letter of each column in the Japanese syllabary "a, ka, sa, ta, na, ha, ma, ya, ra, (wa, wo, n)" appear on the buttons next to the numbers 1 to 10 (see Figure 3–1). The letters are selected by the number of times we press the buttons.

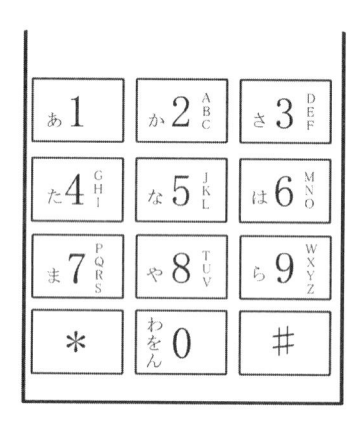

Figure 3–1 Buttons on mobile phones

For example, if you want to enter "sakura", you must press "sa" once to select "sa", press "ka" three times in order to select "ku", and press "ra" once to select "ra". We can do this because the Japanese letters are organized into the Japanese syllabary.

3–2 The value of the Japanese syllabary

The Japanese syllabary is used widely now —— for organizing names to take attendance at school, telephone directory, etc., but its original shape was formed in the Heian era, and it was based on the Sanskrit sound chart of ancient India. The Japanese Buddhist monks brought back the sutras of Buddhism and chart to Japan, who risked their lives to travel to India in order to learn the precept of Buddha (the propagandist of Buddhism in India).

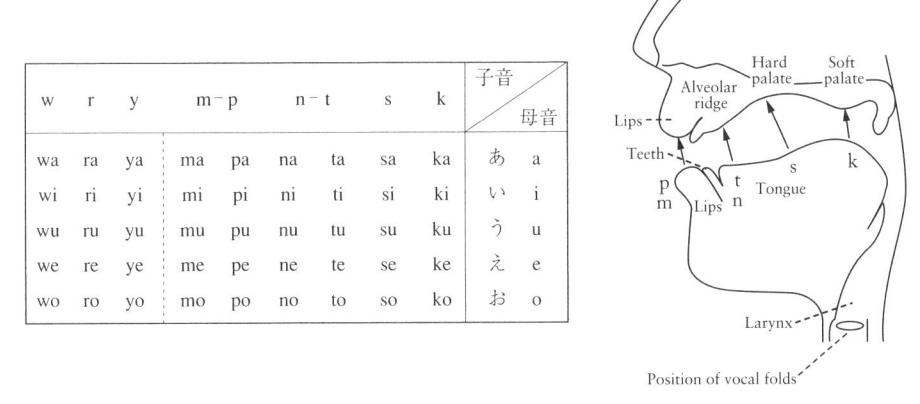

w	r	y	m−p	n−t	s	k	子音
							母音
wa	ra	ya	ma pa	na ta	sa	ka	あ a
wi	ri	yi	mi pi	ni ti	si	ki	い i
wu	ru	yu	mu pu	nu tu	su	ku	う u
we	re	ye	me pe	ne te	se	ke	え e
wo	ro	yo	mo po	no to	so	ko	お o

Figure 3–2 Japanese syllabary, consisting from a set of consonant and vowel, are legitimately aligned in the order of place of articulation from back to front

The Japanese syllabary displays the combination of sounds by placing the vowels on the vertical axis and the consonants on the horizontal axis. It is an enumeration of syllables, and it is important in the way that it shows the full picture of Japanese morae. The fact that Japanese vowels and consonants are organized in rows and columns comes in handy when organizing Japanese in a methodical way. It also plays a role when using machines and computers in order to organize information.

The Japanese syllabary clearly shows the system of Japanese sounds, and it is an effective basic data for education that concerns speech. It may be used for explaining the relation of vowels and consonants, as well as for Japanese education in elementary schools and Japanese education for foreign students.

Moreover, it may be an excellent material for speech training because it is organized into a chart with vowels on the vertical axis and consonants on the horizontal axis. The teaching method may be adjusted according to the age of students, so that learning will be effective and fun. It is most important that children enjoy moving their mouth and tongue, and understand the system of sounds by actually producing sounds for themselves. It should not be about memorizing. Learning will be fun if they are able to say "Aha!" That is most important.

In the kana chart, the three important vowels are placed at the beginning, and the other two vowels are placed at the back. Consonants are placed according to the place of tongue when producing the sounds —— from back to front position. In this way, the Japanese syllabary is excellent phonetic material. It is like sitting on a gold mine. If the syllabary is thought of as only material for teaching letters, it is not too much to say that it will be a great loss to Japanese education.

3-3　The system of Japanese syllabary

The vowels are placed on the vertical axis in the Japanese syllabary. As mentioned before, the three important vowels "a, i, u" are placed at the beginning, and the intermediate sounds "e, o" are placed at the back. The horizontal axis starts from "a", proceeding to [ka], [sa], [ta], [na], [ha], and [ma].

The [ha] line is expressed as [h] today, but it is said that it used to be a weak [p] (or somewhat like [f]) in the old days. Here, it will be expressed as [p]. The data below shows the evidence of this.

"Hahaniwa nido ahitaredomo, chichiniwa ichidomo ahazu"
("Naso" in Gonaraingyosen, 1516)

There is a Japanese saying, that actually is try for English also: "I see my mother twice, but I do not see my father once" What does this mean?

The answer is "lips". The lips meet twice when you say "haha" (mother), but none when you say "chichi" (father). By this, it means that "haha" in this day was pronounced more like "papa". Just for the record, "papa no papa" (mother's mother) is "baba", and "chichi no chichi" is "jiji".

The place of consonants in the kana chart has meaning as well. The first line starts with the sound [k] ("ka" line) when the tongue position is most far back, and proceeds to [s] [t] [n] [p] [m] as the tongue in the mouth moves from back to front. Please try pronouncing them yourself, and feel the tongue move from back to front.

The sound [k] (the "ka" line in the kana chart) is made by using the back of the tongue. The sound [s] (the "sa" line in the consonant chart) is made by narrowing the alveolar ridge and producing frication with the exhalation of air. The sounds [t] (the "ta" line) and [n] (the "na" line) are made at the same place of articulation. The pronunciation of the "ha" line is originally a bilabial [p] sound. Each sound in the "ka, sa, ta, na, pa (ha), ma" lines are set in the order of the place of articulation from the back to the front of the mouth.

The "ya, ra, wa" lines are somewhat like appendices, so to speak. The sounds [y] and [w] are similar to vowels, and therefore called semi-vowels. For the sound [y], the tongue moves toward the back, forms the mouth shape of "i", and quickly moves to "a". [w] is a labial sound, where the lips are in the form of [u], and quickly move to [a]. Neither of the two sounds have all five vowels. The sound [r] is made by flipping the alveolar ridge by tongue tip.

The three sounds "ya", "ra", and "wa" are set in the order of the place of articulation from the back to the front as well; "ya" is made rather at the back, "ra" is a flap sound made at the alveolar ridge, and "wa" is a labial sound.

3–4 Japanese accent and its symbols

The following symbols show the Japanese accent.

The line above the letter shows that its pitch is high. The ⌐ symbol, on the contrary, shows that the next letter will have a low pitch. ○ is a symbol for one vowel, or one mora formed with a set of one consonant and one vowel, and ● is a symbol that shows it has an accent.

Example:

A sa hi   →   a ⌐sa hi, ○⌐○○, ●○○, high-low-low
sa KU RA →   sa ku ra, ○○○, ○●●, low-high-high
a SI TA   →   a si ta ⌐wa, ○○○⌐, ○●●, low-high-high

Sometimes there is a descent or ascent within the ○ depending on dialects, and it may be shown as ◐ or ◑.

Example:
A me → ○◐

When you hear "Ame (rain) has a high-low accent", you would probably think that "A" is high and "me" is low, therefore "Ame" is simply high "A" and low "me". Likewise, "aME (candy)" has a low-high accent; therefore you may simply think that the accent rises from low to high, like climbing up the stairs. It may sound like it when you hear the sounds with your ears, but humans cannot suddenly change the pitch of the voice. It sounds like the pitch is changing fast, because the time it takes to change the pitch is so short. If you look at the change of pitch closely, you are able to see that its change is gradual.

3–5 English sounds and the alphabet

The structure of Japanese sounds is either "one vowel" or "one consonant + one vowel", but the structure of English is somewhat more complex since there are many cases where there are several consonants.

In English, there are five alphabetical letters that correspond to each vowel. The five letters "a, e, i, o, u" are in the order of appearance in the alphabet. You may think that both Japanese and English has the same five vowels, but even if you count the English monophthongs [ɑ ɔ ə ʌ æ e ɛ i ɪ u o] you can see that it has a lot more vowels compared to Japanese. Some vowels that are distinguished in English are thought of as the same in Japanese, so it is quite confusing for Japanese native speakers.

The following words include some of the vowels mentioned above.

[ɑ] h<u>o</u>t (American English) [ɔ] h<u>o</u>t (British English) [ə] broth<u>e</u>r
[ʌ] c<u>u</u>t   [æ] h<u>a</u>t   [e] b<u>e</u>st
[ɛ] <u>a</u>rea   [i] stud<u>y</u>   [ɪ] k<u>i</u>d
[u] b<u>oo</u>k   [o] l<u>ow</u>

Japanese English learners often have trouble with English consonants. Japanese consonants are shorter in duration as well as weaker compared to English consonants. Therefore, Japanese native speakers must consciously pronounce English consonants clearly when speaking in English. When several consonants are present, it is especially important to pronounce each consonant clearly. For example, when pronouncing the word "strike", each sound in [str] ([s], [t], and [r]) must be pronounced so that they can all be heard clearly. The final [k] must also have a clear burst.

3–6 Features of English accent and its symbols

English accent can roughly be divided into primary (´) and secondary (`) stress. It is used as ìntonátion, and there are three ways of transcription, including no transcription.

Some claim that there are four ways to transcribe accent (Bloch and Trager, 1942; Trager and Smith, 1951). Others claim that each syllable in a spoken English utterance can be assigned a numerical stress (accent) level.

Primary stress (´)
Secondary stress (^)
Tertiary stress (`)
Weak stress (˘)

There are primary, secondary, and tertiary stresses in the words óbjĕct, ŏbjéct, cóntènt, and cŏntént. In the case of a group of words like tâll bóys, primary and secondary stresses are used. In this book, the author will use primary and secondary stress.

In both Japanese and English, it may seem like individual sounds are short but they each have their own unique duration. The pitch changes in a very short period of time. The experimental results show the importance of observing such changes. Let's look deeply into it in the next chapter.

CHAPTER 4:

History of accent and the traditional way of thinking

> The word "accent" is a loanword that must be written with *katakana*. However, the accent of Japanese in the Heian era is more or less understood by what is called "sho:ten (accent symbol)" written in an old dictionary. It also shows the historical and geographical correspondence of accent, and is an important aspect of research concerning twentieth century Japanese.
>
> The essence of accent, on the other hand, is as though Japanese has a high-low accent, and English has a stress accent. So how are they different, and have you ever actually learned about them? One of the aims of this book is to unveil the similarities and differences of Japanese and English accents.

4–1 Dialectal accent in Japanese and its history

There is a side story to the famous tale of "Ikkyuusan".

When Ikkyuusan was about to cross the bridge, there was a sign that said "Kono hashi wataru bekarazu (You shall not cross this bridge)".

Ikkyuusan thought this was a trick, and walked right in the *middle* of the bridge (bridge=hasi), not on the edge (edge=hashi).

In spoken speech, "hasi (bridge)" and "hasi (edge)" will be distinguished because their accent is different. In "hashi wo (bridge)", "shi" has a high pitch. In "hashi wo (edge)", the beginning is a little low, and the latter is flat.

The meanings differ depending on which part has a high pitch. We distinguish meanings of words by changing the pitch of our voice.

The examples above are of the Tokyo dialect, but accent differs according to places. The setting of "Ikkyuusan" is Kyoto, so the sign on the bridge must have said "kono HAshi (bridge) watarubekarazu" with a high pitch on the "HA", and "kono HASI (edge) watarubekarazu" with a high pitch on both "HA" and "SI". The accent in Kansai, including Kyoto, is the same today – "HAshi wo (bridge)" and "HASI WO (edge)".

There are certain rules concerning accent. You will be able to use them correctly if you understand the rules of accent in different places.

The old dictionary "Ruijuumyougishou" written about the accent at the end of the Heian era is a famous piece of literature in accent research. Today, research has unveiled the mystery of historical and geographical correspondence of Japanese accent (Kindaichi, 1944, etc.).

The key is the groupings of words called "lexicon classification". Words with two *kanas* are classified into five groups according to the differences in accent. Accents of various regions may fall roughly into these five categories.

"Kaze (wind)" and "hashi (edge)" are in Group 1, "oto (sound)" and "hashi (bridge)" are in Group 2, "hana (flower)" and "ashi (foot)" are in Group 3, "matsu (pine)" and "hashi (chopsticks)" are in Group 4, and "ame (rain)" and "aki (autumn)" is in Group 5. The words in each group have the same or similar accent in any place. The reason remains unknown. The following table shows the words and examples for each group.

Group	Words	Example
Group 1	kaze (wind), hana (nose), hashi (edge), mizu (water), kuchi (mouth), ebi (shrimp)	Kaze ga tsuyoi (The wind blows hard)
Group 2	oto (sound), hashi (bridge), kami (paper), ishi (stone), uta (song), kawa (river)	Oto ga kikoeru (I hear the sounds)
Group 3	hana (flower), iro (color), inu (dog), ashi (foot), oya (parent), yama (mountain)	Hana ga saiteiru (The flower is blooming)
Group 4	matsu (pine), hashi (chopsticks), kata (shoulder), fune (ship), obi (band), sora (sky)	Matsu ga mieru (I see the pine)
Group 5	ame (rain), nabe (pot), saru (monkey), aki (autumn), koe (voice), haru (spring)	Ame ga furu (It is raining)

Figure 4–1 shows the accent patterns according to regions.

(1) shows the Tokyo accent, and (2) shows the regions of Kansai accent. (3) shows the regions for Type 2 accent, which is a region that has only two types of accents no matter how many morae are in each word. (4) is a no accent type, where the accent is not decided on each word. It basically means you can pronounce the word with any kind of accent.

(1) Tokyo accent

Similar to Tokyo accent

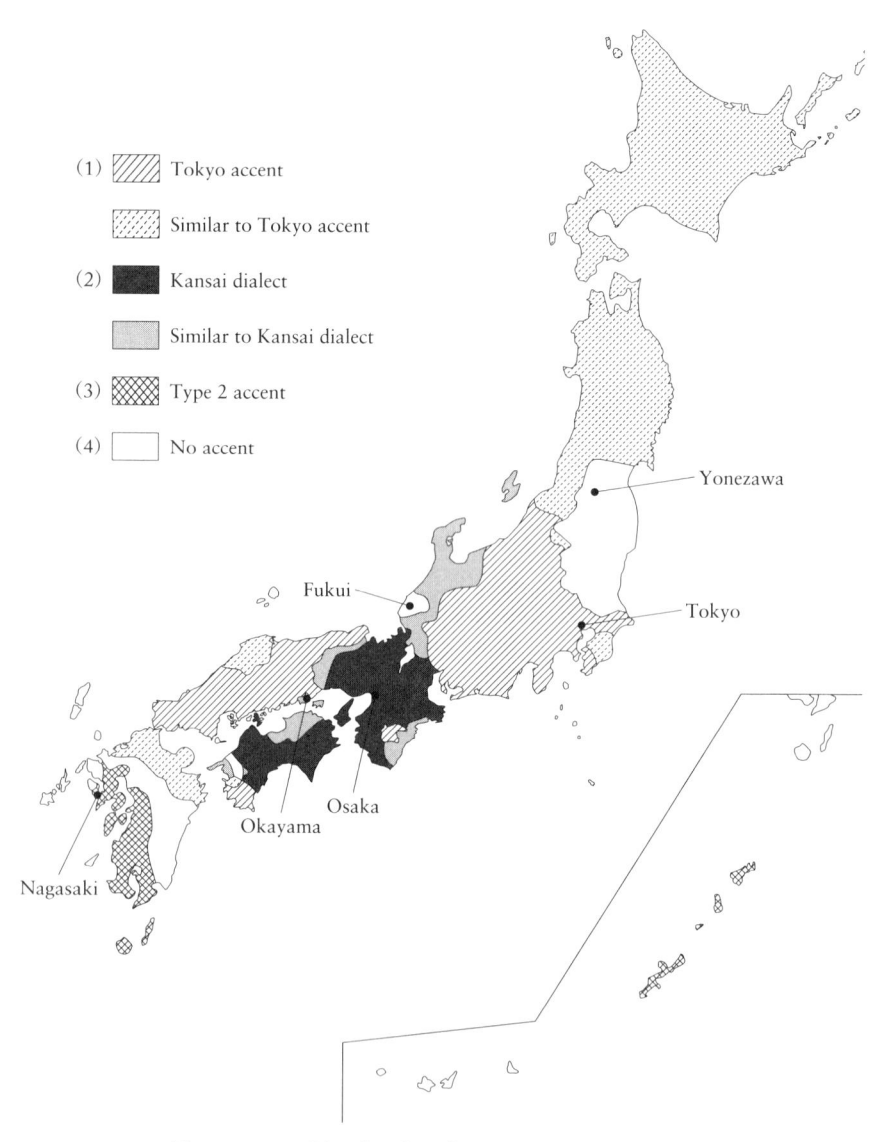

(2) Kansai dialect

Similar to Kansai dialect

(3) Type 2 accent

(4) No accent

Figure 4–1   Distributional map of dialectal accent

The following are examples of Tokyo, Kyoto, and Kagoshima dialects as representatives of different accents according to regions.

(1) Tokyo accent
    Type 1 "kaZE GA tsuyoi" (kaZE = wind)
    Type 2 "oTO ga kikoeru" (oTO = sound)
    Type 3 "haNA ga saiteiru" (haNA = flower)
    Type 4 "MAtsu ga mieru" (MAtsu = pine)
    Type 5 "Ame ga furu" (Ame = rain)

In "kaze", "ze" is a little higher than "ka". In "oto", "to" is higher, and "na" is higher in "hana". When pronounced with the word alone, "haNA" and "oTO" are low on the first mora and slightly higher on the second mora. In Type 2, it becomes "haNA ga" and "oTO ga" when "ga" is added. In Type 1, it becomes "kaZE GA" and "haSHI GA". "Ma" is higher in "matsu", and "a" is higher in "ame".

As Figure 4–1 shows, the accent used in Tokyo accent is used widely across regions.

(2) Kansai accent
    Type 1 "KAZETSU yoi" (KAZE = wind) KAZEGA
    Type 2 "Oto kikoeru" (Oto = sound) Otoga
    Type 3 "HAna saiteru" (HAna = flower) HAnaga
    Type 4 "maTSU mieru" (maTSU = pine) matsuGA
    Type 5 "aME furu" (Ame = rain) aMEga

The level accent in Kansai dialect is high from the beginning to the end. Type 1 "KAZE GA tsuyoi", Type 2 "Oto", and Type 3 "HAna" are high on the first mora and low on the second mora. The high positions are the opposite from Tokyo accent.

The second mora "tsu" is high for words like "maTSU" where the first mora is low, but the accent slides to the back as in "matsu GA" in the middle of a phrase or sentence. Similarly, the first mora is low as in "aMEe (rain)" and high in the second mora, then descend immediately (falling accent pattern).

In a phrase or sentence, "me" has a high pitch as in "a ME ga". The important accent such as "Ame" is unfortunately changing in the young generation into "aME" (low-high).

Also, the Kansai accent was the former standard accent of Japanese.

(3) Accent of Kagoshima dialect
  Type 1 "KaZEno tsuyoka (tsuyoi)" (KAze = wind)
  Type 2 "oTOno suu (suru)" (Oto = sound)
  Type 3 "hana NO secho (saichoru)" (haNA = flower)
  Type 4 "matsu NO miyu (mieru)" (maTSU = pine)
  Type 5 "ame NO fuQ (furu)" (aME = rain)

There are only two types of accent. Type 1 and 2 have the same accent, with the second mora being slightly high, and the rest descends. Type 3, 4, and 5 are different, and the accent is slightly high for mora with accent.

CHAPTER 4: History of accent and the traditional way of thinking

Please pay attention to "tsuyoka" and "suu". The accent is different when they are pronounced alone or within a phrase or sentence. In a phrase or sentence, the accent position slides back by one mora. Interestingly, there are only two types of accents in Kagoshima and Nagasaki even if in a lengthy word.

(4) No accent type

There are no rules in voice pitch in words like in the examples above. The meanings do not change no matter what accent one may use in the no accent regions. The regions are shown in white in the map.

> Column 3: Accent in the people in dramas
> —— Kansai accent and Heian era accent

Kansai accent used in Kyoto, Osaka, Nara and Wakayama maintains the accent used in the political center of the Heian era. If Murasaki Shikibu was to record the Tale of Genji after a thousand years, the accent should be somewhat similar to the Kansai accent of today. Kansai accent used to be the standard accent of Japanese for a long time. If there was a drama based on the history around Meiji era, the accent used by the people of Choshu may be substituted with Tokyo accent, Kagoshima's Type 2 accent for Saigo of Satsuma and Okubo, Kochi accent for Ryoma Sakamoto (Polivanov called this ancient accent "the Sanskrit of Japanese"). The court noble (called Kugyo) spoke with the standard accent of that

Table 4–1 Historical and geographical relations of Japanese accent

所属単語	京都・大阪・奈良 古代	京都・大阪・奈良 現代	東京	鹿児島 長崎
第1類 飴・風・端・鼻・姉・牛・枝・柿・庭・箱・口・水	アメ HH 飴 ●アメ	アメ HH (アメガ)	アメ ⓪ (アメガ)	アメ (アメガ)
第2類 蝉・村・橋・石・歌・垣・川・音・冬・町・雪・牙	セミ HL 蝉 ●セミ	ハナ HL	ハナ ②	
第3類 花・波・池・垢・家・色・岸・草・櫛・耳・山・雲	ハナ LL 花 ●ハナ	(ハナガ)	(ハナガ)	アメ (アメガ)
第4類 海・息・箸・板・今日・糸・稲・船・空・針・松・何	ウミ LH 海 ●ウミ	ウミ LH (ウミガ)	アメ ①	
第5類 雨・声・琴・鶴・春・窓・蜘蛛・朝・赤・猿・秋・牡蠣	アメ LD 雨 ●アメ	アメ LD (アメガ)	(アメガ)	

アメ	→	a me
セミ	→	se mi
ハナ	→	ha na
ウミ	→	u mi
ガ	→	ga

表中の声点（アクセント記号）の意味

▉□	→	High	(O̅)
•□	→	Low	(O)
•▉□	→	Fall	(Ô)

CHAPTER 4: History of accent and the traditional way of thinking

time —— Kansai accent. Yoshinobu Tokugawa spoke with a Tokyo accent in Edo, and the people in each region spoke with a dialectal accent shown in the following table. The regional differences of language may have played a role in creating a sense of patriotic spirit in the people of Meiji era.

4-2 Observing sound waves

It is not so difficult to observe sound waves nowadays if one records the sounds and uses an analysis software. You can also change the waves into a pitch con tour instantly, and observe how voice pitch is changing. All this may be done in an instant today, but it seems as

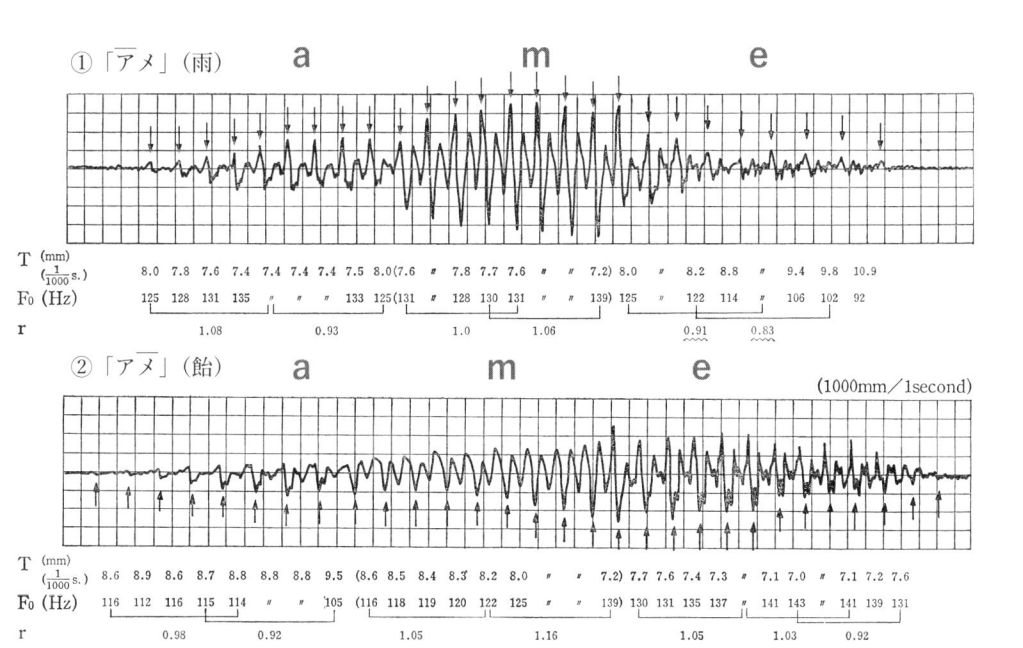

Figure 4–2 Example of an expanded acoustic waveform showing how to extract the voice pitch from the vowels and the consonant in the sound waves of [a-m-e] by measuring the distance between each glottal cycle (successive peaks in the acoustic signal)

though one cannot really see the essence of speech in such ways.

It is like solving a mystery —— one has to use his/her eyes and hands to observe waves, duration, intensity, and pitch. Let's look into it from the beginning. The author believes, from experience, that this is essential to understand the essence of speech.

Figure 4-2 shows the accent of "Ame (rain)" and "aME (candy)" in Tokyo accent. The black arrows show peaks in each wave. The part that says "interval, t (mm)" with an arrow shows the interval between each wave, in other words, the length of each wave. Calculating the reciprocal of the length will show the pitch (Hz). The amount in Hz will be obtained by measuring each wave one by one.

If you compare the fourth value (Hz) with the first three, you will see whether the voice pitch is rising, declining, or staying flat. You will see how much the contour is rising or declining if you look at the proportion of the value. I went through these stages to understand the essence of accent by observing the change in voice pitch for each word.

The parts with short intervals have fast vocal folds vibrations, which means the pitch is high. The parts with a wide interval, on the other hand, mean the pitch is low. In "Ame (rain)", the interval of arrows becomes wider at the end, whereas in "aME (candy)", it becomes shorter. This means that "Ame (rain)" has a falling intonation at the end, and "aME (candy)" has a rising intonation at the end.

The unit used for pitch is Hertz (Hz). This is called the fundamental frequency (F0), which shows how many times vocal folds vibrate per second. The contour that shows the changes in pitch is called a pitch contour.

CHAPTER 4: History of accent and the traditional way of thinking

"Ame" ('rain') and "aME" ('candy') in Tokyo dialect

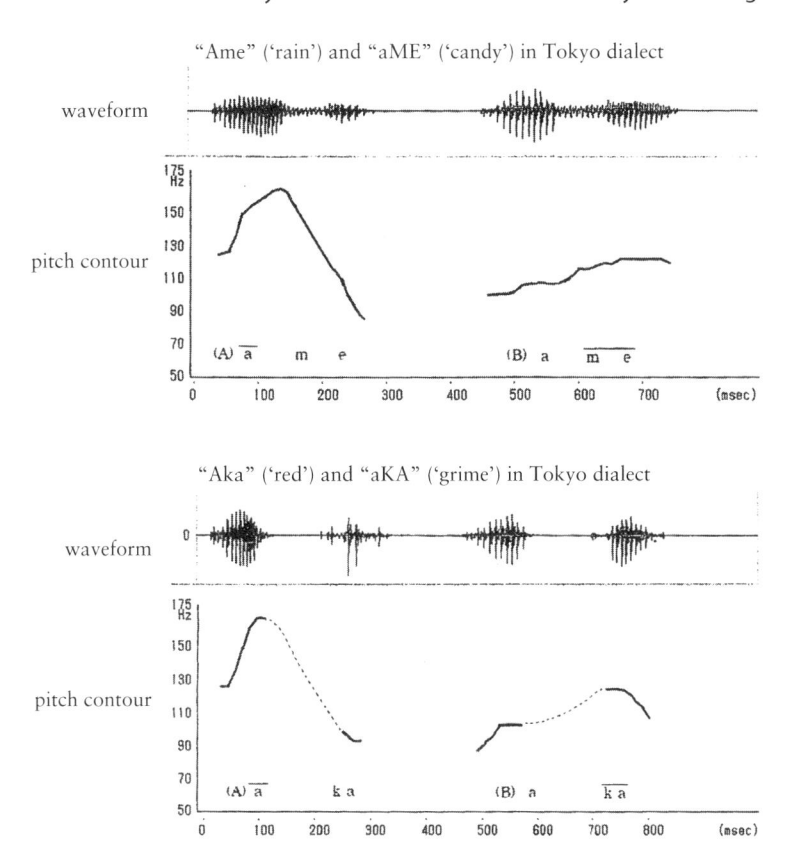

Figure 4–3 Waveforms and pitch contours of "ame" and "aka"

Figure 4–3 shows the sound waves and pitch contours of "Ame (rain)", "aME (candy)", "Aka (red)", and "aKA (grime)" spoken in Tokyo accent.

The [m] sound in [ame] is a voiced consonant, so the pitch contour is continuous. The [k] sound between vowels in [aka] is a voiceless consonant, so the pitch contour is cut off. Please see the difference in the continuous vocal fold vibrations for the voiced consonant, and no vibration for the voiceless consonant.

> **Column 4: Accent of Totsukawamura**

Let me go back to the story of the ancient times —— People lived on the islands of Japan in the Jomon era. Some may have travelled from south in the course of hundreds of years. Others may have travelled from north. There were people who came later and became policymakers, who may have travelled across China or Korea. Many may have stayed in the Kansai area. The accent of "aMEe" that have been introduced in this book many times may have been created in such course of time.

Totsukawamura, which has the largest area from north to south, is in Nara, once flourished as the capital. There is a long bridge that crosses over a mountain stream, which you will be too frightened to look down upon. It is a rarely visited region that people once carried people and objects across the valley by using baskets woven with vines called "Yaen".

The voice of the patriarch sounded like our ancestor in northern Kanto or Tohoku area the first time I heard it. It was Japanese with Tokyo accent (Katsuji Fujioka, a former professor at the University of Tokyo, first discovered that Tokyo accent was used in that region). Such prosody is spread across the east and west of Japan such as the area close to Japan Sea, Kanto, and Tohoku. Totsukawamura is close to the central area, but in the out-country of deep valley. It is natural that language in such area is preserved in its original form, even after people like policymakers came in. This was the place of a story of Emperor Jinmu travelling north with the lead of a three-legged crow.

Maybe the change and propagation of Kansai accent, the original form of Japanese, did not spread and change into Tokyo accent, etc., as scholars once claimed.

4–3 How accent was apprehended

The differences in the accent of Japanese and English were thought of as typical as in the following examples. Please try to see what the problem is in the following passage.

CHAPTER 4: History of accent and the traditional way of thinking   41

Accent is on the first mora in "hashi (chopsticks)". If you move it to the second mora, it becomes "hashi (bridge)". If you pronounce "coffee" with a gradual rising intonation on the second syllable, it becomes an interrogative. The first syllable has a higher intensity. The second syllable is higher and the first syllable has high intensity when you say "coffee?" Japanese has a high-low accent, and English has a stress accent. (Kindaichi, 1967)

The passage is confusing pitch and intensity.

It says "The second syllable is higher and first syllable has high intensity when you say "coffee?" ", but the second syllable is not simply "higher" but gradually becomes higher. It has a rising intonation. Additionally, the first syllable "co" in "coffee" may be high but not necessarily with intensity.

Voice pitch changed within 5/1000 ~ 10/1000 second of vowel production when "hashi (chopsticks)" and "hashi (bridge)", "hashi (chopsticks)?" and "hashi (bridge)?" is produced in Japanese, and when word accent moves to the second mora in English such as in "cóffee" [káfi] and [kafí], "coffee?" [káfi↑] and [kafi↑].

When the accent is on the second syllable, the vowel in the second syllable rises and then falls. The difference between "cóffee" and "coffee?" is on the second syllable.

The author observed the changes in the vowel and interrogative intonation of various two-syllable words that accent changes its form to nouns and verbs (for example, "accent" and "object"). The rising and falling intonations are only a part of the actual condition, and the pitch contours look something like what is shown in Figure 4–4. As the arrows pointing upwards show, the pitch contours for interrogatives are rising.

(1) shows "Ame" (left) and "aMe" (right) in declarative and interrogative forms spoken by a male Kansai dialect speaker, (2) shows

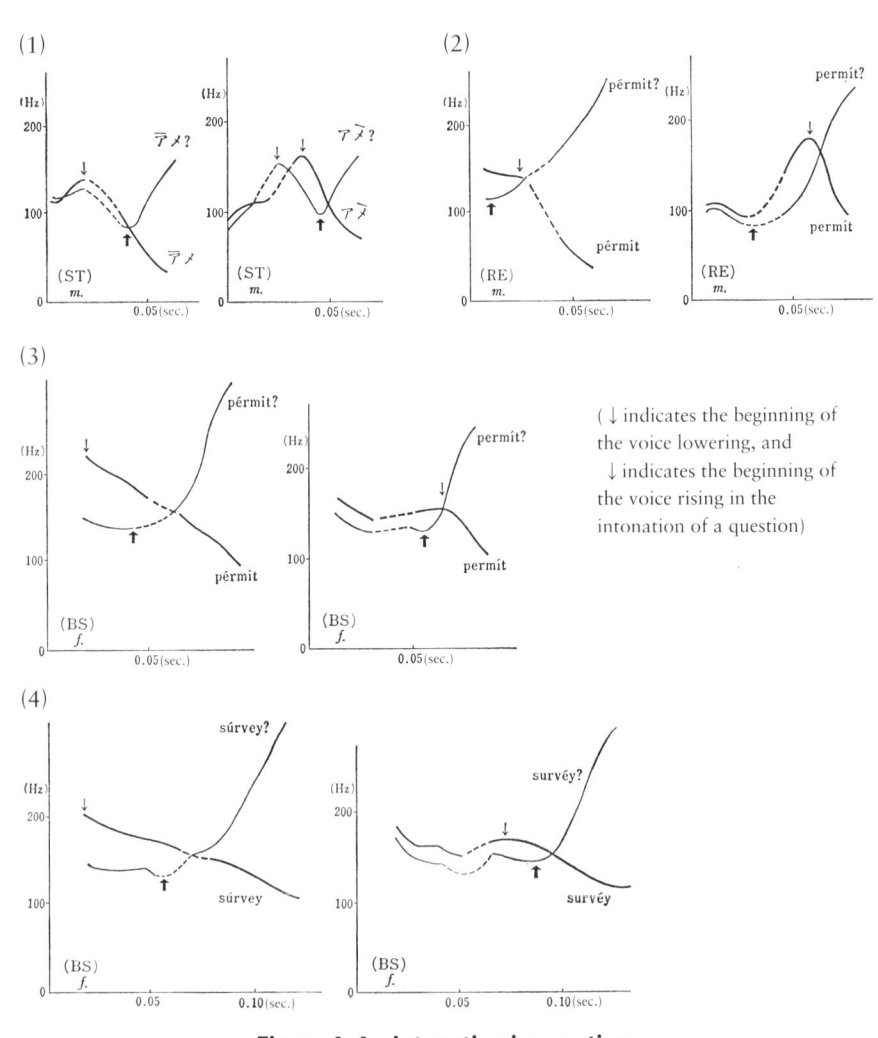

(↓ indicates the beginning of the voice lowering, and ↑ indicates the beginning of the voice rising in the intonation of a question)

Figure 4–4 Intonation in questions

CHAPTER 4: History of accent and the traditional way of thinking

"pérmit (left) / permít (right)" in declarative and interrogative forms by a male English native speaker, (3) shows "pérmit (left) / permít (right)" in declarative and interrogative forms by a female English native speaker, and (4) shows "súrvey (left) / survéy (right)" in declarative and interrogative forms by a female English native speaker.

Please look at Figure 4–5. (1) shows the differences of (a) "hashi (chopsticks)" and (b) "hashi? (chopsticks?)" in Japanese, (2) shows the differences of (a) "hashi (bridge)" and (b) "hashi? (bridge?)" in Japanese. In the example of English, (1) shows the differences of (a) "coffee" and (b) "coffee?"

(1) ⓐ箸 ⓑ箸？　hashi (chopsticks)　(2) ⓐ橋 ⓑ橋？　hashi (bridge)

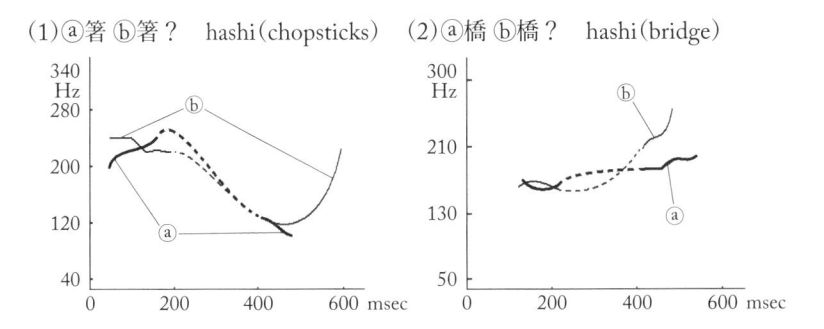

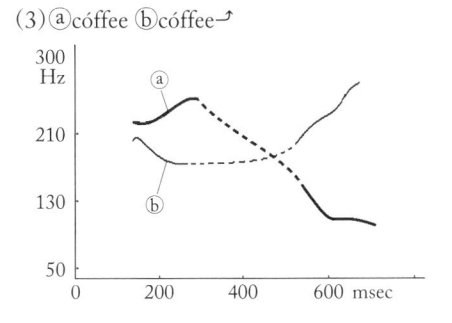

(3) ⓐcóffee ⓑcóffee↗

Figure 4–5 Tokyo accent Japanese (1) a. "HAshi" ('chopsticks') b. "HAshi?" (2) a. "haSHI" ('bridge') b. "haSHI?" English (1) a. "coffee" b. "coffee?"

If you compare "hashi (chopsticks)" and "hashi? (chopsticks?)", the interrogative form becomes "HAshi↑" whereas the declarative form is "HAshi". The second mora "i" has a rising intonation. This is not a high-low-high accent, but rather a high-low-rise accent.

"Hashi (bridge)" in an interrogative form has a rapidly rising vowel in the second mora, as in "ha↑shi" (low-rise). The high accent is in the second mora in the case of word accent, but the final vowel gradually rises in interrogative form.

> **Column 5: Accent and intonation**
>
> Lexical accent is acquired at an early stage, when infants begin to take in sounds with meanings into the brain. Words with meanings (=words) are taken in as a chunk of sounds, and the accent is also accompanied to it and set into the brain. Accent is included in the output as well. Sometimes infants make mistakes in the sounds and accent, and they notice their mistakes and try to pronounce it again. Such cases were clearly observed in the production of speech sounds in infants by myself (Sugito, 2005). Intonation, unlike word accent, differs in each production. The changes are due to emotion, intention of the speaker, and nuances that have an influence on the voice pitch (but the word accent does not change). Intonation conveys the intention of the speaker to the listener. Interrogative forms have a rising intonation in many languages. The changes in the voice pitch are called intonation as well.

4–4 Difference between "hanakago (flower basket)" and "hana kago (flower and basket)"

Let's observe the boundaries in continuous speech. For example, what is the difference between a compound word "hanakago (flower basket)" and "hana (flower) / kago (basket)" which has a boundary? Traditionally, it has been said that the difference is in how intense the first mora of the following word is produced (Hattori, 1960). However, a number of experimental results showed that it is not decided by the intensity but rather by the change of voice pitch of the following word (Sugito, 1996). (Please refer to "tall boys" below.)

In the case of "hanakago", [na] in "hana" is high, and "kago" gradually falls. When there is a boundary between the two words, [na] in "hana" is high, [ka] is low, and the vowel in "go" is flat and does not fall. When the two words are continuous ("hanakago"), [ka] and on and after will have a falling intonation. In this case, the accent is on "na" as in "haNAkago" (Sugito, 1973).

How about in English? How are compound words "tall boys" and "tall, boys" with a boundary between the two words different?

If you raise your voice pitch at "tall" and bring it down on "boys", the two words will sound continuous. "Tall, boys" with a boundary between the two words (indicated here by a comma) have a high pitch at the beginning for both "tall" and "boys", and then lowered. Boundaries and continuity may be distinguished by changes in intonation for both Japanese and English. Numerous measurements have revealed that accent is distinguished by pitch, not intensity. When vowels have a falling intonation, we perceive an accent on the previous syllable in both Japanese and English. Therefore, it seems we cannot simply say that "Japanese has a high-low accent, English has a stress accent".

The next section will organize past research on English accent, and how it has previously been recognized.

4–5 Brief history of English accent

(1) Perceptual loudness, amplitude of sound waves, and intensity of speech

Many linguists thought of accent as perceptual loudness. Also, Bloomfield (1933) thought of accent as amplitude of sound waves. Jones (1909, 1932), Palmer (1924), Armstrong (1926), etc. thought of it as 'force of utterance' or 'breath force'.

Jones (1909) compared each syllable of a record and described the temporal relation between syllables. He clearly distinguished accent and intonation, which are independent at the articulation level. He also claimed that perception of accent is performed through the feedback of the speaker's production (1932). We could say that this was the start of the later "analysis-by-synthesis" (Stevens, 1960).

(2) Duration

Fry (1955) and Bolinger (1958)'s experiments, however, overturned the notion of "accent and prominence (emphasis) is intensity".

First, Fry measured the duration and amplitude of sound waves in the sounds of pairs differing in accent such as óbject / objéct and cóntract / contráct. Perceptual experiments were conducted based on the measurements, and results revealed that duration and amplitude do play important roles in perceiving accent, but duration carries more weight. Lengthening [ɔ] or [e] in "object" distinguishes óbject / objéct. This experimental finding gave the idea to people that duration is important in accent, and it became a common notion.

(3) Pitch

Bolinger found by experiment that the pitch of a sound is important in English accent. He investigated cases of increasing the intensity of pitch of vowels in expressions such as 'Br*ea*k both *a*part' by using synthesized speech. As a result, he states that pitch is far more effective than intensity in perceiving accent. The factor that emphasizes the accented syllable is the prominence of pitch, plus addition of extra duration and intensity to it.

(4) Analysis and synthesis by computer

The technique of speech analysis and speech synthesis has gone through massive progress with the development of computers. As research in automatic speech recognition advanced, however, acoustics shifted to a more time-consuming phonetics research, and revealed that human speech does not correspond simply to linguistic symbols. The view of word accent research has also shifted its interest from simple intensity to duration, pitch, and quality.

Lindblom (1963) claimed that accent is determined by duration and vowel quality. Vowels without an accent have shorter duration, and "vowel neutralization" occurs because articulation of the next sound begins before features of vowel quality reach its target values.

Liberman (1967) viewed that pitch was the most important factor for accent perception, although vowel duration and amplitude also has influence.

In terms of speech perception, Liberman and Cooper (1962) presented the "articulatory reference theory" which refers to one's own articulation at the level of nervous command. The modeling of Analysis-by Synthesis (Stevens, 1960) has also been carried out in the process of perceiving and recognizing speech. Speech mechanism was modeled based on this theory, and synthesized speech was used for verifying speech perception.

As an example of accent research, Öhman (1967) set up a model for speech mechanism on pitch and acoustically explained the dialectal accent of Swedish. In terms of English accent, there was an approach that adopted pitch as the main factor in the rules of accent in synthesized speech (Mattingly, 1966), and also an approach that proposed that pitch is the most important factor (Cheung, Holden, Manifie, 1977).

Let's look at some of the characteristic phenomena of Japanese accent.

CHAPTER 5:

"Late fall" and "accent on voiceless mora"

> There are various views on Japanese pitch accent. How about the cases of "late fall" and "accent on a voiceless mora"?
>
> The heart of the problem becomes prominent when you conduct experiments and observe the durational changes in the pitch contour. Japanese does in fact have a pitch accent. The problem is whether you can explain the exceptions.

5–1 "Japanese has a pitch accent" —— is this really true?

It has been said that Japanese has pitch accent. There also have been views that there are too many exceptions to state this is really the case.

First and foremost is research by Tsutomu Chiba and Masato Kajiyama (1942), well-known for their research on vowels. Chiba also did an experiment on the pitch and intensity in words and sentences of nine languages. He concluded that Japanese, like other foreign languages, involves changes in pitch and also changes in intensity

(Chiba, 1935).

The next work to be introduced is Neustupný's theory of "late fall" (1966). In the preface, he states: "What should be paid attention to is that the essence of Japanese accent has never been proved by experiments":

> Experiments have shown there are many cases of "late fall". This means that the mora <u>after</u> the lexically accented mora has a higher pitch than the lexically accented mora. Therefore, one must conclude that Japanese accent cannot be explained by pitch only. As described by Chiba, intensity must also be taken into consideration. (Neustupný 1966)

Chiba's 1935 research paper about the importance of intensity in Japanese accent was to be published in the Journal of the Phonetic Society, so I was told to read the paper before discussing about Japanese accent. The following is another view on the "late fall". The first mora in the Tokyo dialect, if it is not High, is Low. Because of this feature, the first mora of a word becomes Low. This is called "late fall" (Fujimura 1967). However, such a "late fall" is also observed also in the Kansai dialect which does not have this accent rule. Moreover, in the Kansai dialect, a word may start with either an H or L accent. And, in the Kansai dialect "late fall" can be observed in many words with an accent on the first mora, such as "KUsa (grass)", "KUse (habit)", and "SHIta (tongue)".

What about accent on voiceless mora? It has been said that it is impossible to explain this phenomenon. For example, in the Tokyo dialect, the mora "shi" as in "haSHI to kawa (bridge and river)" is accented but is devoiced at the same time. Regarding this phenomenon, whereby an accent falls on a voiceless mora that has no vocal fold vibration, it has been said that this is because of the falling pitch of the following vowel. However, this was disproved by Kanae Sakuma's (1929) experiment.

The following two questions arise.

(1) Is it true that "Japanese cannot be said to have a pitch accent" because there are many cases of "late fall"? How do we interpret the cases of accent on voiceless mora?
(2) Is it true that we should consider not only pitch but also intensity when we think about accent?

5–2 What is "late fall"? ⸺ Is intensity a factor?

How do we answer Neustupný's view that "we cannot say that Japanese has a pitch accent because experiments have found many cases of 'late fall' in Japanese"?

Out of 556 words spoken by a Tokyo dialect speaker, there were 36 three-mora words Of these 36 words, nine had a lexical accent on the first mora.

(a) **A**tari   (b) **NA**sake   (c) **YU**taka   (d) **KA**rasu   (e) **TA**nuki
(f) **YA**shiro   (g) **NI**kusa   (h) **YA**mai   (i) **SA**wagi

The phenomenon of "late fall" was observed in three of the nine words (a, b, and c). The mora after the accented first mora has a higher pitch than the lexically accented mora.

Figure 5–1 shows examples of "late fall" in "**NA**sake", "**YU**taka" and "**A**tari". (The capitalized, bold letters indicate the lexical (phonological) accent. Although lexically, the pitch accent is on the first mora, phonetically, the high pitch is on the second mora. This is called late fall.

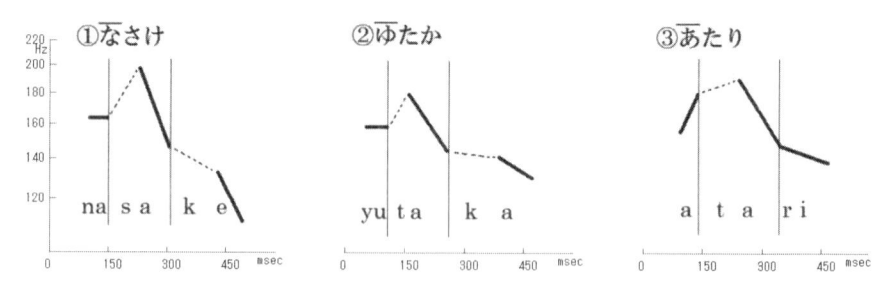

Figure 5–1   Examples of "late fall": "na-sake", "yu-taka" and "a-tari"

There are some common points in the three words "nasake", "yutaka" and "atari". The first mora is a vowel, or a voiced consonant that is close to a vowel (nasal [n] and semi-vowels [y] [w] are considered to be close to vowels). The second mora is made of a set of "voiceless consonant + [a]".

5–3   What does "accent on a voiceless mora" mean?

It is usually thought that "sutoraiku" has five morae. In regions other than Kansai, however, the first and fifth morae become devoiced as in [su̥toraiku̥]. Recently, there is a tendency for this even in the Kansai area.

Vowels [u] and [i] are likely to be devoiced between voiceless consonants such as [s] [t]. In the case of "sutoraiku", [u] in voiceless moras [su] and [ku] become devoiced. In such cases, there is no voice produced because there is no vocal fold vibration. This is called vowel devoicing.

It is often the case that the speakers themselves do not notice that they are devoicing the vowels. This is why they still count the vowel as one mora, even though there is no vowel.

There is an exception to the rule of vowel devoicing. For instance, "shibashi (for a while)". The accented first mora tends to undergo devoicing, even though the [i] vowel in this mora is followed by the voiced consonant [b], not a voiceless consonant. The case of "shibashi" will be discussed further in Chapter 7.

In the Tokyo dialect, the following words have devoiced first mora and the accent is on the second mora.

(a) "ku̥SA (grass)"   (b) "ku̥SE (habit)"   (c) "ki̥TA (north)"
(d) "fu̥SA (bunch)"   (e) "hi̥TO (people)"   (f) "shi̥KA (deer)"

Now let's look at the Kansai dialect. These words have accents on the first mora in Kansai dialect, and usually are not devoiced. However, recently, the first vowel may be devoiced, and is often produced as "KUsa", "KUse", and "KIta".

> **Column 6: Accent of "sankakkei (triangle)"**
>
> "Sankakukei (triangle)" is often pronounced as "sankakkei". The accent is on the fourth mora, but the fourth mora is a geminate, and, therefore there should not be any vowel sound. However, to the Japanese ear, it sounds like there is an accent on this geminate mora. The final "kei" has a falling pitch, as shown in Figure 5-2 (although the NHK "Accent Dictionary" shows three patterns "saNKAkukei", "saNKAKUkei", and "saNKAkkei"). The assessment of pitch is decided by the pitch movement on the following mora. This means that listeners perceive an accent on the mora preceding a falling pitch.
>
> The description in the dictionary does not put an accent on voiceless mora, indicated with a small circle below the devoiced sound, and geminates. However, there is an accent on the devoiced "ku" in the second pattern "saNKAKUkei". "SaNKAKUkei" and "saNKAkkei" is only a matter of different interpretation. "kei" has a falling pitch, so listeners perceive an accent on the fourth mora.

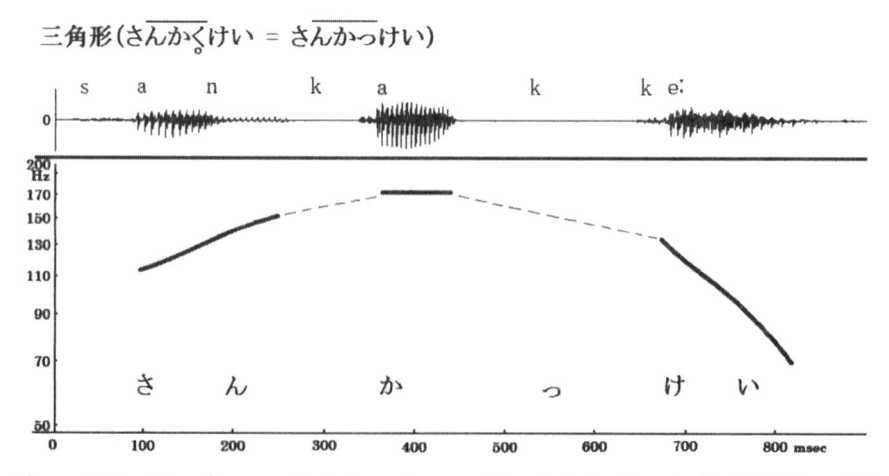

Figure 5-2 Waveform and pitch contours of "sankakukei (sankakkei)" ('triangle')

5–4   The cause of "late fall"

There are no voiceless consonants in the first mora of "nasake", "yutaka" and "atari". The words begin with either a vowel, a nasal [n], or glide [y], and the second moras "ta" and "sa" begin with the voiceless consonants [t] or [s], followed by the open vowel [a].

The pitch at the beginning of an utterance has the following features.

(a) Moras or syllables that begin with a vowel or voiced consonants [n] [m] [d] [g], [y] [w] have a low pitch, as exemplified by [atari] [nasake] and [yutaka].

(b) Syllables that begin with voiceless consonants ([k] [s] [t]) as in the second mora in the three words, have a high pitch on the following vowel. If you take a look at the sound waves, you will see that the first wavelength of the vowel following the voiceless consonant is fairly short—which means that the pitch is high.

The accent pattern of High-Low-Low is seen in words such as in [atari] [nasake] [yutaka], which begin with a vowel or a voiced consonant. The pitch first starts off low, and becomes higher on the second mora, so the vowel of the first mora has a rising pitch. The second mora starts off high, then falls, due to the influence of the voiceless consonants [t] and [s]. Because of this, the beginning of the second mora, rather than the accented first mora, has a higher pitch.

The "late fall" phenomenon is shown in Figure 5–1.

When the first mora that is supposed to be high has a rising pitch from low to high, the second mora starts off high then falls because it begins with a voiceless consonant. Thus the first mora has a delayed rise. The first mora that begins with a vowel begins with a low pitch and rises, and the second mora which begins with a voiceless consonant begins with a high pitch and then has a delayed fall.

The first mora in [atari] is the vowel [a], not a voiceless consonant, so the first mora starts at a low pitch, then rises. If the pitch becomes high enough by the end of the first mora, the phonetic pitch contour will correspond to the lexical accent pattern. However, the rise in the first mora is delayed and the vowel in the second mora that begins with [t] starts off high, so the word will have a falling pitch (the mora preceding the mora with a falling pitch is perceived as a high pitch). This phenomenon is natural for words that begin with a vowel or a voiced consonant, but it has no relation to stress.

5–5   What is an accent with a falling pitch?

Words with a Kansai accent such as "aka↓(red)", "ame↓(rain)", "haru↓(spring)", "aki↓(autumn)", "tsuru↓(crane)", and "kame↓(turtle)" have existed since ancient times in the Kinki region. They are historically categorized as Type 5 accent pattern (see Chapter 4).

The falling pitch of this accent pattern gave me a clue about "late fall" and accents on voiceless mora. This also played an important role in comparing the lexical accents of Japanese and English.

In 1906, E. A. Meyer (from Uppsala, Sweden) experimented and analyzed words with a falling pitch pattern such as "tsuru↓(crane)". Thus, figures from the Meiji era were preserved (Meyer, 1906). A Kyoto-born associate professor (at the time) at the University of Tokyo, Shoji Fujioka, was the participant of the experiment. The figures show the pitch contours of two-mora Kyoto-dialect words. The figures are very clear, and show the Kyoto-accented "**TSU**ru (chord)" (Figure 3), "**TSURU** (fish)" (Figure 4), and "tsu**ru**↓(crane)" (Figure 5). This was the first time Japanese was used as the experimental material, and therefore the figures are extremely valuable (Sugito, 1982).

The Russian scholar, Polivanov, arrived in Japan in 1914, after being inspired by Meyer's work. He had already studied the Tokyo accent, and had access to the "Encyclopedia of Japanese" by Taketaro Yamada (1892) (also known as the writer Bimyo Yamada). This encyclopedia included accent marks on all the words.

Table 5–1 is an excerpt of Polivanov's paper on dialectal accents (1928). Nagasaki, a region with a Type 2 accent, deserves particular attention.

In 1978, I travelled to Miemura, Nagasaki, in order to record the voice of Ei Iwa who had once met Polivanov. She was an old woman by that time, but she was only 18 years old when Polivanov had visited Miemura. According to Ei, Polivanov had come to Miemura during summer vacation with Ei's older brother who was studying at a university in Tokyo. The phonetically transcribed nursery tale "Hanasakajiji" (the old man who makes flowers bloom) spoken in

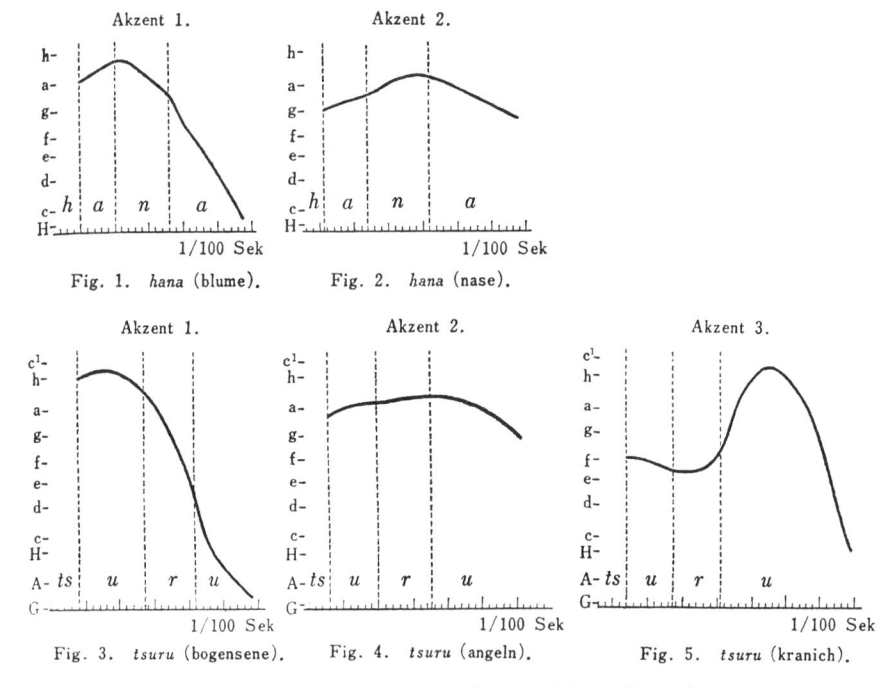

Figure 5-3 Experiment by E. A. Meyer (1906)

Tokyo accent: Fig. 1 "HAna" (name of a person; written with the Chinese character meaning 'flower') ("haNA":'flower' as in the plant, written in the same Chinese character as in the name of a person), Fig. 2 "haNA"('nose').
Kyoto accent: Fig. 3 "TSUru" ('string'), Fig. 4 "TSURU" ('fishing'), Fig. 5 "tsu↓ru" ('crane') (falling intonation).

Miemura dialect is preserved (Murayama, 1976).

As reported in Sugito (1982), Polivanov first discovered the correspondence relations between the Kyushu Type 2 accent and other accent patterns. He was an excellent researcher and his work, which started the research of Japanese accent, is of great importance.

The historical and regional patterns of Japanese word accent and the accents of Kansai, Tokyo, and Kyushu are arranged in a perfect framework, showing the corresponding relations of the dialectal

Table 5–1 Correspondence table for dialectal accent in Japanese

2 mora words	Kyoto	Tosa	Tokyo	Nagasaki
鼻、牛、柿、蟹、金、皿、竹、口	┌ハ ナ┐ ha na	┌ハ ナ┐ ha na	── ハ ナ ha na (ハ ナ ガ) ha na ga	ハ ナ┐ ha na (ハ ナ ノ┐) ha na no
行く、着る	┌イ ク┐ i ku	┌イ ク┐ i ku	── イ ク i ku	ハ ク┐ ha ku
花、猫、池、栗、時、豆、雲	┌ハ ┐ナ ha na	┌ハ ┐ナ ha na	ハ ┌ナ ha na (ハ ┌ナ ガ) ha na ga	ハ ┌ナ ha na (ハ ナ ┌ノ) ha na no
(麻)、笠、喉、甕、白、海、今、屑	カ ┌サ ka sa (カ サ ┌ガ) ka sa ga	カ ┌サ ka sa (カ ┌サ ┌ガ┐) ka sa ga	カ ┌サ ka sa (┌カ サ ガ) ka sa ga	カ ┌サ ka sa
飲む、切る	ノ ┌ム no mu	ノ ┌ム no mu	┌ノ ム no mu	ノ ┌ム no mu
朝、錫、亀、葛、影、蜘蛛、猿	ア ︿サ a sa (ア ┌サ ガ) a sa ga	ア ┌サ a sa (ア ┌サ ガ) a sa ga	┌ア サ a sa	ア ┌サ a sa

Made by Sugito (1982) based on Polivanov's description

accents (see Table 5–1). The important point here is that the accents of Kansai and Tokyo, as well as the Type 2 accent pattern of Nagasaki and Kagoshima, show good correspondences. As for the other dialectal accents, Teruo Hirayama (1940, 1957) and other researchers conducted field research in various regions including Kyushu, and discovered details of dialectal accent around the country. Shiro Hattori (1931–33, 1951) later organized the corresponding relations of the main dialectal accents. On the other hand, Okumoto Inoue (1916) showed that accent symbols existed along with an ancient dictionary "Ruijuumyougishou". Haruhiko Kindaichi (1943, 1974) researched and organized the accent symbols of ancient times, and summarized the corresponding relations between dialectal accents.

Please see the reference at the end of the chapters for more details.

5-6　The unexpected discovery!

—— Let's pay attention to the similarities between Kansai word accent with a falling pitch, and English word accent

"ame↓(rain)" and "aka↓(red)" (F accent) have a unique accent pattern. This pattern with a falling pitch is important in that it gives us a clue to discover the similarities with English accent.

For example, the English word "fatigue" has an accent on the "ti", but if you observe closely you will find that "fa" is low, the beginning of "ti" in "tigue" is high, and then suddenly declines. I realized that it had the same pitch as "aka↓(red)" (F accent) when the pitch contours of "fatigue" and "aka" are overlaid. I noticed that this was an important discovery and conducted numerous experiments. Let's look at English two syllable words and Japanese two mora words. If you connect the first syllable, say of the English word, with the second mora of the Japanese word, (or vice versa), then you can synthesize a word that has an accent which sounds very natural—in either Japanese or English. Of course, the word has no meaning, but it sounds like it might be Japanese or English.

I once made synthesized speech for word accents in Kansai dialect by using Densuke, an open-reel recorder from SONY. It was in the times when there were no computers, so synthesizing was done by cutting and pasting the actual tapes used for recording.

Synthesizing could be done by splicing a tape, not only to make a Japanese word or an English word, but also by cross-splicing, one could synthesize a "Japanese-English hybrid word". The following is an example of the procedure. It may seem complex, but you can do it all on the computer today, so let me explain in detail!

<Experiment 1>
<Connect "-tésque" in "grotesque" after "ka" in "kaki (oyster)". "ka" has a low pitch in Kansai dialect, so it becomes "katésque". "ka" in Tokyo dialect has a high pitch, so connecting it with English "-tésque" will make a compound word "kátesque". Similarly, connecting a low-pitched "ka" of "kaki (persimmon)" after English "-tigue" of "fatigue" will make "katígue".>

If you cut out [ta] from "**TA**ko" or" ta**KI**", and put it right before the second syllable of the English words "récord" or "recórd", then you get either "**TA**-cord" with a high pitch at the beginning, or, "ta-córd", that starts off low then becomes higher. It will sound very much like English. Of course, the gender of the speaker as well as the voice quality should be considered.

In any case, the accents sounded natural. Therefore, the following conclusion may be drawn.

(1) If the following mora has a falling pitch, the pitch of the preceding syllable (mora) will be perceived as high. Therefore, it sounds like the accent is on the first syllable (mora).

(2) The word accent of English, as well as in Japanese, is judged based on pitch movement.

It is not accurate to say that accent is decided by stress in English and pitch in Japanese. Although it has been said that Japanese has a lexical pitch accent while English has a lexical stress accent, these are not completely different from each other. Both are essentially the same type of accent phenomenon.

When pitch falls from High to Low within a vowel, the accent is perceived on the preceding syllable, and in that respect, English and Japanese are similar. It can be concluded that the decisive cue in perceiving word accent is pitch movement. This experiment showed that it is possible to explain accent as a whole if you take particular note of pitch movement. It is because I had gone through a huge amount of troublesome manual work such as measuring fundamental frequencies and cutting and pasting of tapes.

> **Column 7: Kansai accent of "Ame (rain)" with a falling pitch**
>
> Kansai accent may be divided into two types: one that begins with a high pitch, and the other that begins with a low pitch. In addition, there is a type of accent that has a falling pitch on the second mora such as "ame↓e (rain)", "aka↓a (red)", "haru↓u (spring)", "aki↓i (autumn)", and "asa↓a (morning)". This strange type of accent plays an important role in the present research. In the case of "a" in "ame↓e (rain)", the pitch is low at the beginning, the second mora is high at the

beginning, and then lowered right away. In other words, this word has a falling pitch. Please try pronouncing it! This kind of rise and fall within a vowel is observed in Chinese and Thai, but in Japanese, it is only observed in the Kansai accent, as in one-mora words with rising accent type "e↑ (picture)" and falling accent type "ha↓(leaf)", and in two-morae words like "ame↓e (rain)" with a Low-HighLow accent type. (This type of pitch accent can also be seen in the Nakijin region of Okinawa). This Kansai accent led me to the insight that Japanese accent and English accent, which have been considered to be completely different, show similar patterns. of the chapters for more details.

CHAPTER 6:

How do English native speakers perceive Japanese accent?

> Although Japanese has been said to have a pitch accent, there are many cases of "late fall" examples, and there are "unreasonable cases" where there are accents on voiceless mora.
>
> English has a stress accent —— do native English speakers perceive Japanese accent as Japanese native speakers do?
>
> I conducted perceptual experiments with English native speakers to verify this point. Based on the experimental results, this chapter discusses the basics of English accent.
>
> As has been pointed out several times, the unit of speech for Japanese is the mora, and the syllable for English. It is difficult to compare the two since the rhythm is different. For the sake of simplicity and convenience in comparing the two, they will both be treated as mora-rhythm languages.

6–1 Experiment on how English native speakers perceive Japanese accent

The examples of "late fall" in words "atari↓", "nasake↓", and "yutaka↓" in the previous chapter clearly have a higher pitch on the second mora compared to the first. However, experiments with Japanese native speakers have shown that they perceive the first mora higher than the second.

How would English native speakers perceive the same sounds? Also, would the Japanese phenomenon of perceiving accent on voiceless mora without vocal fold vibration also occur with English native speakers? I therefore performed perceptual experiments with English native speakers using the words "yutaka", "atari", "nasake", and some other words.

The first participants were four American listeners, two who had lived in Japan for seven years. Participant R.E. was fluent in Japanese. Participant S.E. also had no trouble with Japanese. The other two (Mr. & Mrs. W) were visitors who heard Japanese for the first time when they arrived in Japan. The wife was good at playing the piano, and was acquainted with music. However, Mr. W could not write the answers, and was not able to continue so his results were excluded. In the end, there were only three participants.

Table 6–1 shows the answers of the three American participants.

The words "yu↓taka", "a↓tari", and "na↓sake" in Table 6–1 have "late fall" with the second mora higher than the first.

The experiment showed that not only Japanese, but also English native speakers who heard Japanese for the first time, also perceived accent on the first mora.

The second mora following the first has a falling pitch, but the syllable that precedes the syllable with falling pitch is perceived as a

Chapter 6: How do English native speakers perceive Japanese accent?

Table 6-1 Results of perceptual experiment

Results of Japanese accent perceptual experiment (3 times each) by native English listeners. (①~③ on the left are words with "late fall" intonation, where the accented first mora is not higher than the second mora)(Please refer to Figure 5-1 for "late fall" pitch contours.)

Participant / Experiment / Word	RE (Mr.) experiment 1	experiment 2	experiment 3	RE (Mrs.) experiment 1	experiment 2	experiment 3	LW experiment 1	experiment 2	experiment 3
あなた	anáta	anáta	anáta	anáta	anáta	anáta	anáta	anáta	anáta
① なさけ	násake	násake	násake	nasáke	násake	nasáke	násake	násake	násake
まよい	majói	majói	majói	majói	majói	majói	majói	majói	majói
えくぼ	ékubo	ékubo	ékubo	ékubo	ékubo	ékubo	ékubo	ékubo	ékubo
ねがい	neŋái	neŋái	neŋái	neŋái	neŋái	neŋái	neŋái	neŋái	neŋái
なたね	natáne	natáne	natáne	natáne	natáne	natáne	natáne	natáne	natáne
② ゆたか	jútaka	jútaka	jútaka	jutáka	jútaka	jutáka	jútaka	jútaka	jutáka
わらい	warái	warái	warái	warái	warái	warái	wárai	warái	warái
③ あたり	átari	átari	átari	átari	átari	átari	átari	átari	átari
しばし	ʃíbaʃi̥	ʃíbaʃi̥	ʃíbaʃi̥	ʃíbaʃi̥	ʃíbáʃi̥	ʃíbáʃi̥	ʃíbáʃi̥	ʃíbáʃi̥	ʃíbáʃi̥

high pitch. It is suggested that this phenomenon is not unique to Japanese native speakers, but also to English native speakers.

The same can be said in the case of [ʃibaʃi̥] with the voiceless first mora. The first mora does not have vocal fold vibration. It is impossible to judge the pitch of the accent. And yet, an accent is perceived on the preceding voiceless mora. In such cases, the following vowel [a] has a falling pitch. This also is an interesting phenomenon.

And this is perceived not only by Japanese native speakers, but also by English native speakers, whose language is said to have a stress accent. This means that English word accent may have features similar to Japanese. In other words, when there are unclear or omitted vowels in an utterance, listeners can still perceive the speaker's intention by guessing the unclear portion by using the pitch of the following portion.

6–2 Features of English accent

Word accent and sentence intonation can be observed by the pitch contours. Pairs of words that differ in accent (nouns and verbs, for example) are shown in Figure 6–1.

Figure 6–1 shows the amplitude (stress) at the top, and the pitch contour (durational change of pitch) at the bottom. Participants (1) to (4) are Americans, and (5) is British. (1) to (5) compare the two-syllable English words "pérmit" and "permít", and (6) compares the Japanese (Osaka) participant ST KAme (jar) and ka↓me (turtle). The arrows above the pitch contour indicates when the pitch starts to fall.

In the case of "pérmit" with an accent on the first syllable, the beginning of the word has an especially high pitch, and then declines after the arrow. On the other hand, "permít" with an accent on the second syllable starts off low on 'per', then the second syllable 'í' is high at the beginning, after which the pitch has a sharp decline.

The change of pitch in the second syllable of "permít" from high to low is similar to the second syllable of "a↓me (rain)" in Kansai dialect. The pitch contours of "KAme (jar)" and "ka↓me (turtle)" in (6) are over-layed, so you can compare them with the English words.

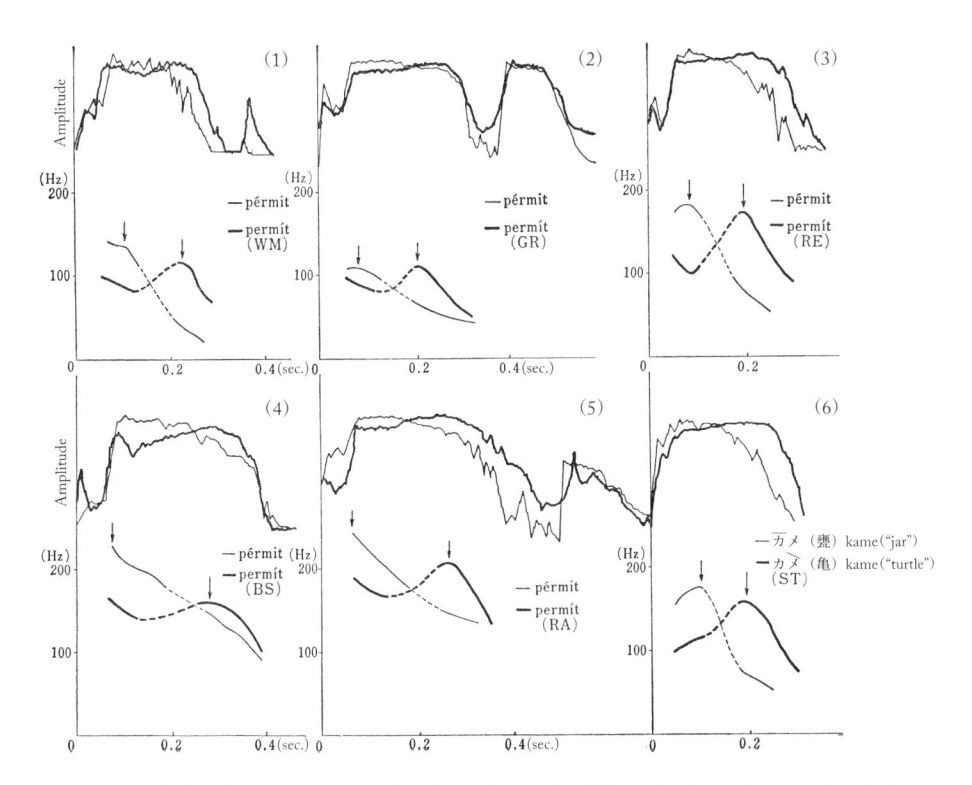

Chapter 6: How do English native speakers perceive Japanese accent? 69

Figure 6–1 Comparison of pérmit and permít, KAme (jar) and ka↓me (turtle)
(Graphs 1-5 show amplitude (intensity) at top and pitch contours at bottom (durational change in pitch) of pérmit and permít by four native American English (1-4) and one British English speakers. Graph 6 shows "KAme"('jar') and "ka↓me" ('turtle') by Japanese speaker ST with an Osaka dialect. Please see that they resemble the example in (3).
The arrows above pitch contours show the starting point of the fall in intonation.

6–3 The nature of Japanese and English accents

We have compared two-syllable words "permit" and two-mora words "kame", hypothesizing that the unit of English rhythm is mora, and not the syllable. If we also hypothesize that the duration of an

English mora is fixed, how would the pitch change? How would it be if the duration of each syllable is fixed, and we then compared each mora and syllable?

The present experiment used four to five mora words for Japanese, and four to five syllable words for English. There were 242 words in Japanese, and 153 words in English. We first extracted the mora or syllable with an accent, and measure its duration. As we investigated the correlation of duration and accent, we found that when the duration is longer there was a higher tendency of perceiving accent in English compared to Japanese,.

It may seem that the tendency for duration to determine the accent is higher for English than Japanese, but this is not exactly so. It cannot be said that "English word accent is determined by duration". We shall discuss this point later.

The next experiment also hypothesized that English consists of mora, not syllables, and that the duration of each syllable is fixed. The voice pitch was investigated for 550 Japanese words and 400 English words by using exactly the same method.

What we found was that in English as well as in Japanese, accent is perceived on the syllable with high pitch, or on the preceding syllable if the vowel has a falling pitch.

The example above does not show exceptional cases. However, the mora after the accented mora is obviously low or has a falling pitch in English. Word accent may be clearly determined by the change of pitch. Words for which the place of accent cannot be determined by this method are only four out of 400 words. It means the exceptions are only 1%. This shows that word accent in English is also determined by voice pitch.

We can conclude that accent is determined by voice pitch and its dynamic change. In particular, accent is perceived when the vowel has a high pitch, or it is perceived on the preceding syllable when the vowel has a falling pitch.

6–4   Duration and pitch of syllables

Figure 6–2 compares the accents of Japanese (Tokyo dialect) and English on the hypothesis that duration of the units (mora or syllables) are the same. There are ten types of accents in the five words in Osaka dialect (shown in III as reference).

The duration of sounds are fixed so that each syllable fits into the dotted lines in the figure.

The results showed the following features. Let's take a look at the Japanese words first.

A. Japanese: The part in the square shows the accented mora. The words were randomly chosen.

① ⟦a⟧   me ga shi ta
② i   ⟦ro⟧ o   ka   i
③ ma   ⟦tsu no⟧ u   chi
④ o   ⟦ni   ba   ba⟧ a

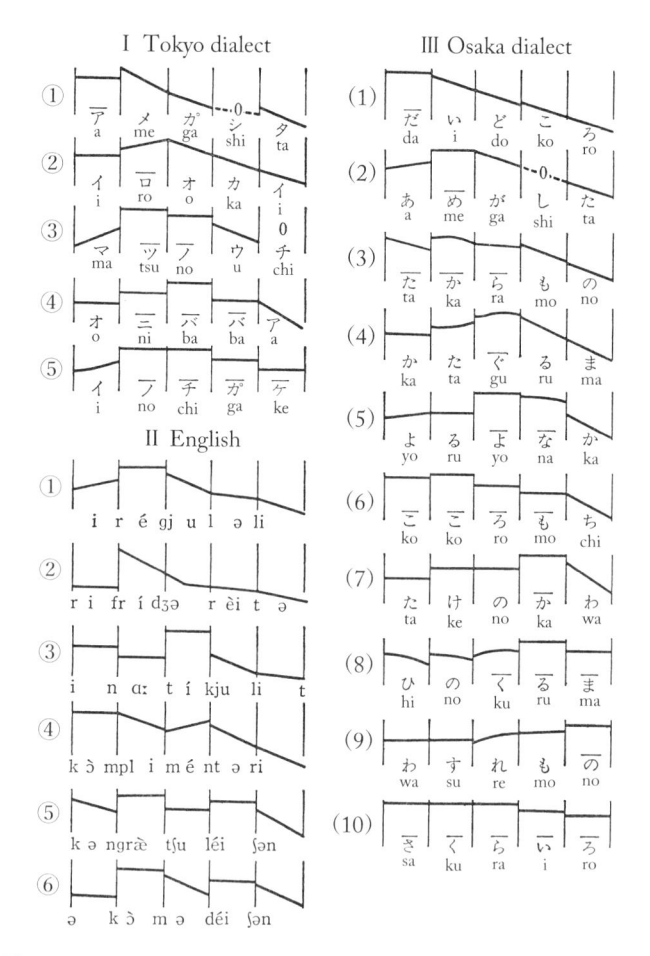

Figure 6-2　Comparison of Tokyo dialect and English accent

⑤ i | no chi ga ke | (level accent)

The following list explains the pitch characteristics.

① "amegashita": "a" with an accent has a high pitch, and the rest "megashita" has a gradual falling pitch.
② "irookai": "ro" with an accent rise and has a high pitch, and the

rest gradually declines.

③ "matsunouchi": "tsu" and "no" are accented and have high, level pitch, "u" has a falling pitch, and "chi" is devoiced.

④ "onibabaa": Each mora has a level pitch until the fourth mora "ba"; the final "baa" has a falling pitch, thus indicating that the accent is on the previous mora "ba".

⑤ "inochigake": Each mora has a level pitch, and the word has a level accent.

The following shows the features of English.

B. English: (´) shows a primary strong accent, and (`) shows a secondary weak accent.

① irrégularly
② refrígerator
③ inartículate
④ còmpliméntary
⑤ congràtulátion
⑥ accòmmodátion

In English, as well as in Japanese, a primary accent is pronounced with a high pitch, and secondary accent is pronounced with a slightly high pitch. All words may be explained by high and low. The following shows a summary for each word.

① irrégularly: "ré" has a high pitch, and then gradually declines. The syllable preceding the declination is accented, just as in Japanese.
② refrígerator: The second syllable "fri" has a falling pitch, and is distinctly high. Other syllables have a low pitch, and the second syllable is accented.
③ inartículate: The third syllable is distinctly high.
④ còmpliméntary: The third syllable "me" has a rising pitch, which makes it distinctly high. The first syllable, which has the secondary accent, is the next highest pitch.
⑤ congràtulátion: The primary accent is on "la", and the secondary accent is on "gra". "gra" is slightly higher than "la", but "la" sounds higher. This is because the end of the word has a natural decline that makes the pitch lower.
⑥ accòmmodátion: The same may be said about "co" and "da". "co" and "da" have a high pitch, and the following syllables have a falling pitch. "da" sounds higher than "co".

6–5　How would you interpret English accent?

If you hypothesize that English has a mora-timed rhythm like Japanese and show that the durations of each syllable are fixed, English word accent can be explained by pitch (see Figure 6–2).

The figure shows the results of arbitrary words, and they clearly show that accent positions in words may be detected by the dynamic changes in voice pitch, and that accents are perceived in the syllable

Chapter 6: How do English native speakers perceive Japanese accent?

that precedes a falling pitch. The same can be said about the other words as well.

The experimental results may be summarized as follows:

(1) 550 words with one to six mora by Tokyo and Osaka dialect speakers were recorded and converted to sound waves. Changes in pitch within a vowel were investigated in detail for each accent. Results showed that perception of pitch in the preceding mora differs according to the dynamic state of pitch, that is, whether the following mora has a flat or falling pitch.
(2) The same analyses were performed on 400 English words. English accent, like Japanese, is determined by pitch, that is, the dynamic state of pitch, to be exact.

These results show that English accent, as well as Japanese accent, is determined by pitch, or fundamental frequency, and that they both hold similar basic characteristics.

This chapter also shows that English native speakers perceive the "late fall", the exceptional cases in Japanese accent, in the same way Japanese native speakers do, and that the perception of accent is similar in both English and Japanese words.

> **Column 8: A gift from a child with golden hair**
>
> I was listening to the recorded sounds of Osaka accent on earphones with Densuke, a recorder for broadcasting stations, on my way to Tokyo from Osaka, and writing down the words under the sound wave columns. This was like my hobby.

The narrow, long roll of paper had a meter of sound waves drawn for each second of speech sound, and they were sent to me in thick rolls. A second of speech is only as long as "It was raining in the morning". I quickly wrote down the words I heard: "asa (morning)", "ame (rain)", "hotaru (firefly)", etc., below the waves.

Just then, I felt a small soft hand touching my hair from the back. I looked back, and saw a small girl with golden hair sitting behind me. Maybe she wanted to touch the black hair that was different from hers. We looked at each other, and smiled. It was a lovely smile. I took off my earphones, and listened to her talk.

She spoke only in words —— in word sentences. The little girl's mother would stop her conversation with her husband, and answer her daughter with word sentences as well. I listened to their conversation, and I, accustomed to looking at sound waves, could see the durational change in the pitch in speech spoken by the mother and daughter. I knew by instinct that English word accent could be solved by the exact same method used for Japanese. I imagined and compared in my head the Osaka dialect speech I was listening to with my earphones, the voices I could hear from behind me, and their sound waves and pitch contours. Yes. I can do it.

I'm going to record speech by English native speakers! For preparation, I bought a small dictionary for working, and started to mark words in it as I took my train home. I will begin with organizing the words that I have looked up, record the English speech just like the way I did with Japanese, interpret the sound waves, measure the wavelength, and observe the dynamic changes in pitch… Hearing the voices of the mother and daughter on the train was what got me started to record English sounds one after another!

CHAPTER 7:

Perception of accent: it is determined by pitch, not intensity!

The phenomenon of "late fall" observed in Japanese accent —— under what conditions does it occur? This chapter will look into how perception works in the cases of accented voiceless morae, and in "late fall" by using synthesized sounds.

Next, I will create 40 synthesized pitch contours in four types of Kansai accent in a joint research, and investigate the perception of accent, and whether accent perception is determined by pitch or intensity.

The targets are the next four points:

(1) Does accent perception change if intensity is increased in the morae or syllables in words?
(2) Does accent perception change if durational position changes in high-pitched parts?
(3) Are there individual differences in accent perception? Are there regional or dialectal differences?
(4) Is accent in English determined by changes in the pitch, just as in Japanese?

> Next, a perceptual experiment on accent was performed with one high school class in each of the six cities that has a different accent type. The residential area and its accent type for each high school student are in the list below. Please also refer to the accent map (Chapter 4, Figure 4–1).

1. Yonezawa city in Tohoku (no accent)
2. Tokyo (Tokyo accent)
3. Fukui city (no accent)
4. Osaka city (Kansai accent)
5. Okayama city (Tokyo)
6. Nagasaki city (Type 2 accent)

Regional differences in accent types were investigated in order to see whether accent perception differs according to region or dialect. Also, influence of education of accent perception will be considered (and whether it can be modified or not).

7–1 Discovering the mystery of "late fall" —— its synthesized sounds

Synthesized speech will be used for the experiments in this chapter. Therefore, I began by creating synthesized speech of "late fall" words.

Please take a look at Figure 7–1. When the first mora is flat, as in (a), (b), (c), (d), and the second mora has a falling pitch as in (e), the words will sound "High-Low type". However, when the first mora is even lower, as in (d), the vowel in the second mora will sound like it has a falling pitch.

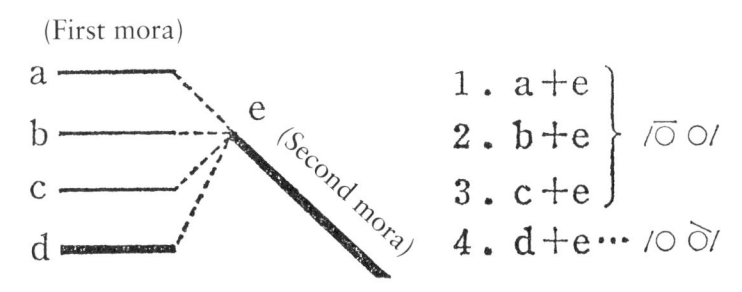

Figure 7–1 Experimental Result 1 from using synthesized sound
Words will be perceived as "high-low" accent, if the first mora does not have an accent (as in a,b,c,d), and the second mora has a falling intonation (as in e), even if the first mora has a rather low pitch. If the first mora is even lower, as in d, the second mora vowel will be perceived as a falling intonation.

You can see that accent is determined by the dynamic state of pitch, or changing pitch of the vowel, and not by the comparison of moraic pitch and intensity.

The intonation of morae and syllables may be roughly divided into two types: ones that are fairly flat in pitch, and ones that have a falling intonation from high to low. In cases of two-mora words (two-syllable words in the case of English), accent is perceived on the preceding mora or syllable when the following mora or syllable has a falling pitch movement from high to low. This is the same for both Japanese and English.

However, when the preceding mora or syllable has a lower pitch than the following mora, the second mora sounds as though it has a falling pitch (for example, "a↓me" in Kinki dialect). In the case of English, it sounds as though there is an accent on the following syllable.

Figure 7–2 compared the stimuli that were manipulated with 19 different pitch variations on the first mora, from "Asa" ("morning" in the Tokyo dialect) to "a↓sa" ("morning" in the Kansai dialect). The short horizontal lines on the slashes that show the pitch of the second mora vowel, show the pitch of the first mora vowel indicate the pitch of the first mora vowel when there are differences in the perception of accent type.

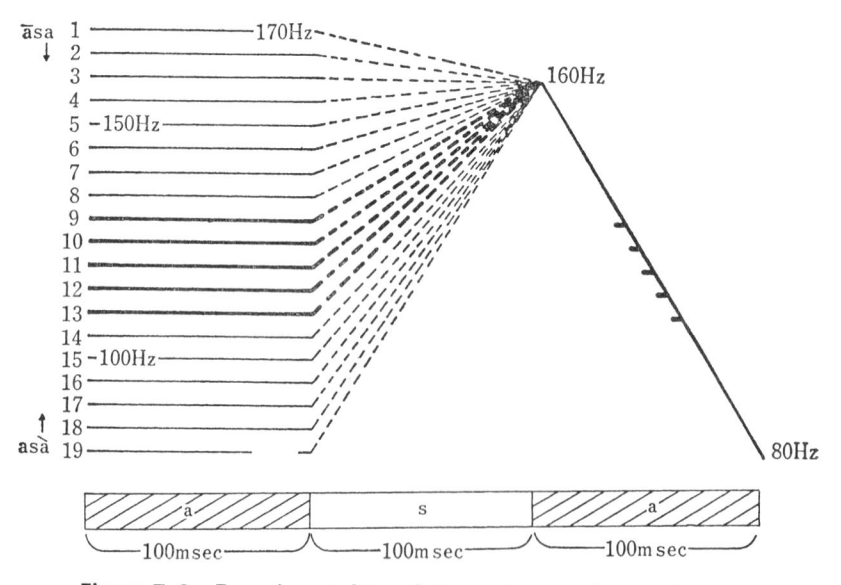

Figure 7–2 Experimental Result 2 by using synthesized sound
From "Asa" ('morning' in Tokyo dialect) to "a↓sa" ('morning' in Osaka dialect) —— word with 19 variations of pitch created for the experiment —— The horizontal lines on top of the diagonal lines that show the pitch of the second mora vowel show the pitch of the first mora vowel when accent type perception is unstable.

CHAPTER 7: Perception of accent   81

Please take a look at Figure 7–2. As the 1 – 19 types of horizontal lines show, the first mora has a flat intonation, and when the second mora vowel after the consonant /s/ has a falling intonation from 160 Hz to 80 Hz, we perceive an accent on the first vowel even if the pitch is low as in #9 to #13.

The figure shows the relation of pitch changes and accent perception, but what is happening here is the phenomenon of "late fall". Please remember that this is not determined by the intensity of the sound, as we have previously discussed.

When the pitch of the first mora is between #9 and #13, as in cases with a lower pitch, the second mora is perceived to have a falling intonation (as in "a↓sa").

Figure 7–3 compares "**Asa**", "**ASA**", and "a↓sa". The heavy lines in the figure show areas that are perceived as (Note: "○○ type" is often used in Japanese, which is more or less the same as "×× type" in

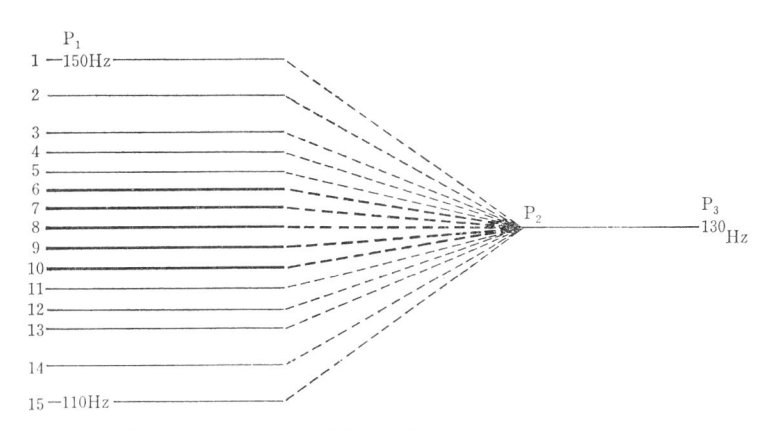

Figure 7–3   Experimental Result 3 by using synthesized sound
/asa/, "Asa" – "ASA" - "a↓sa"
(Bold lines in the figure show the range that will be perceived as "high-high" type accent.)

English), and the second mora has a flat pitch. This avoids the "late fall", unlike in the cases of a falling second mora. Accent is perceived on the first mora, and the pitch range in the first mora pitch will be reduced.

Figure 7–4 shows the example of a synthesized sound of an accented voiceless mora. (1) shows the sound waves and pitch contour of "Asa", (2) shows the sound waves and pitch contour of "kuSA", and (3) shows a combination of "sa" in "Asa" and voiceless mora "ku̥" in "ku̥SA".

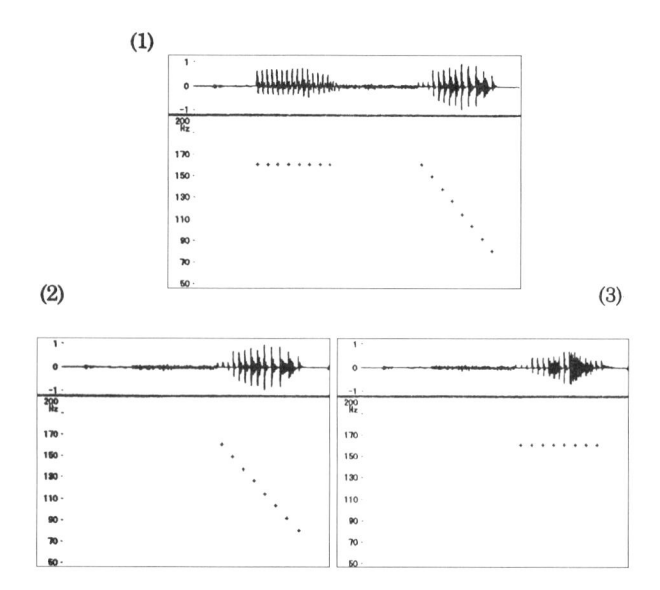

Figure 7–4 Experimental Result 4 by using synthesized sound
(1) Waveform and pitch contour of "Asa" ('morning')
(2) Waveform and pitch contour of "ku̥SA"
(3) "ku̥ " in "ku̥SA" (1) connected to "sa" in "Asa" (2)

Accent will be perceived on the first syllable, even if it is voiceless, when the following (second) mora has a falling pitch as the figure of

(2) shows. The SUGI Speech Analyzer (Sugito, 1996) was used to synthesize and to verify this.

7–2   40 synthesized "ame" based on an accent production model

Basic research on natural speech had been carried out in the 1900s in the field of acoustics. Research advanced to using computers, synthesized sounds began to be used, and methods to synthesize contours that show features of accent also developed.

Models for producing pitch contours were created, and the pitch of actual speech productions were extracted (fundamental frequency contours, to be exact). Next, the pitch contour is analyzed by using mathematical equations of the production model. Speech is synthesized by using the obtained variable.

The Swedish researcher Öhman (1967), for example, made a model for the process of changing pitch in Swedish, a pitch accent language. Given a little twist to it, the production model, shown in Figure 7–5, was created for Japanese accent. This was published in the article "A Model for the Generation of Fundamental Frequency Contours of Japanese Word Accent", Fujisaki & Kudo, 1971. Analysis by speech synthesis was performed.

The contour in Figure 7–5 is a "pitch contour by using voice control mechanism", so to speak.

This is a trapezoid that shows the on and off of voicing in a

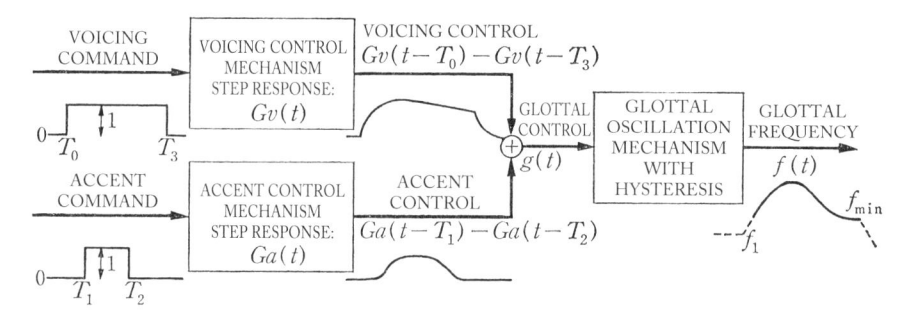

Figure 7-5 A model for the generation of fundamental frequency contours of Japanese word accent (Fujisaki & Sudo, 1971)

phrase, that is, the time at which the vocal folds start and stop vibrating. We shall call this the "accent trapezoid contour".

If you overlay the "accent trapezoid contour" on the pitch contour, the pitch contour of natural speech may be synthesized.

In Chapter 5, the four accent types were explained according to their lexical classifications for two-mora words in the Kansai dialect, but here we will call them Type A, Type B, Type C, and Type D, for the sake of convenience.

The results of analyses may be categorized as follows:

Type A: "Ame" (heaven)   <Group 2, Group 3>
Type B: "a↓me" (rain)   <Group 5>
Type C: "a**ME**" (non-word)   <Group 4>
Type D: "**AME**" (candy)   <Group 1>

As preparation for an analysis of the accent production model, the four accent types listed above were recorded clearly by a Kansai dialect speaker ST (male) at a relatively slow rate. The pitch was

CHAPTER 7: Perception of accent   85

extracted, and the points where we see pitch rises and falls as well as the range of the pitch range were measured for each accent type based on the accent production model. The data were used to create synthesized speech.

Figure 7–6 shows the fundamental frequency contours of the four accent types for the two-mora word, "ame". The "+" symbol indicates the measured pitch values, and the curves with solid lines are the fitted ones by the model. *T1* and *T2* show the beginning and the ending of the accent command, respectively (Fujisaki and Sugito, 1977).

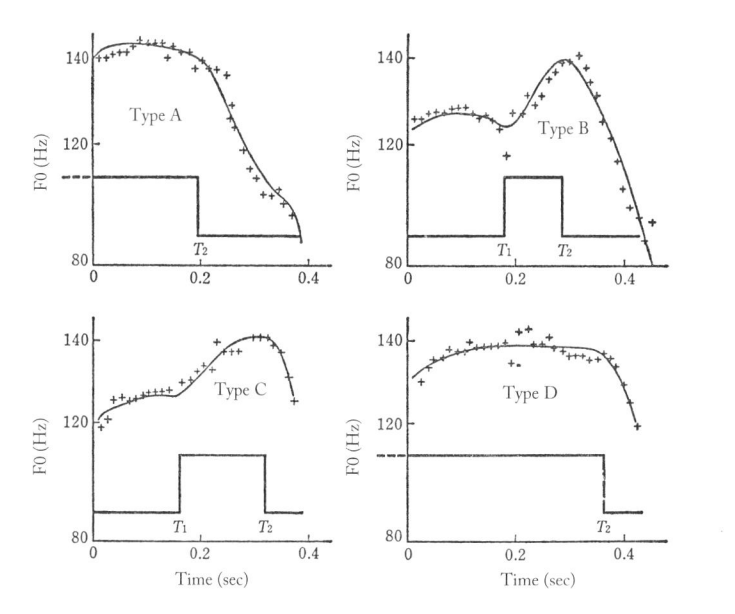

Figure 7–6   Beginning and ending of fundamental frequency and accent command

F0 pattern that shows the four accent type for the two-morae word [ame] (+ symbol shows the measured value, and the contour shows the fitted curve), and the durational positions of the beginning and ending points (*T1*, *T2*) of accent command. (reference: Fujisaki & Sugito, 1977)

Figure 7–7 shows the 40 synthesized pitch contours. The top contour of each column shows the representative pitch contour for each synthesized accent type using variables obtained from analyzing Types A, B, C, and D. The arrows indicate the beginning (↑) and ending (↓) of the accent command.

Each column is numbered from ① to ④. The upper left says "Type A – Type B". The left-most column shows the 11 pitch contours (F0 contours) where the highest part shifted equally to the back, as in Type A "Ame" to Type B "a↓me". The F0 of ① is shown in No.1 –

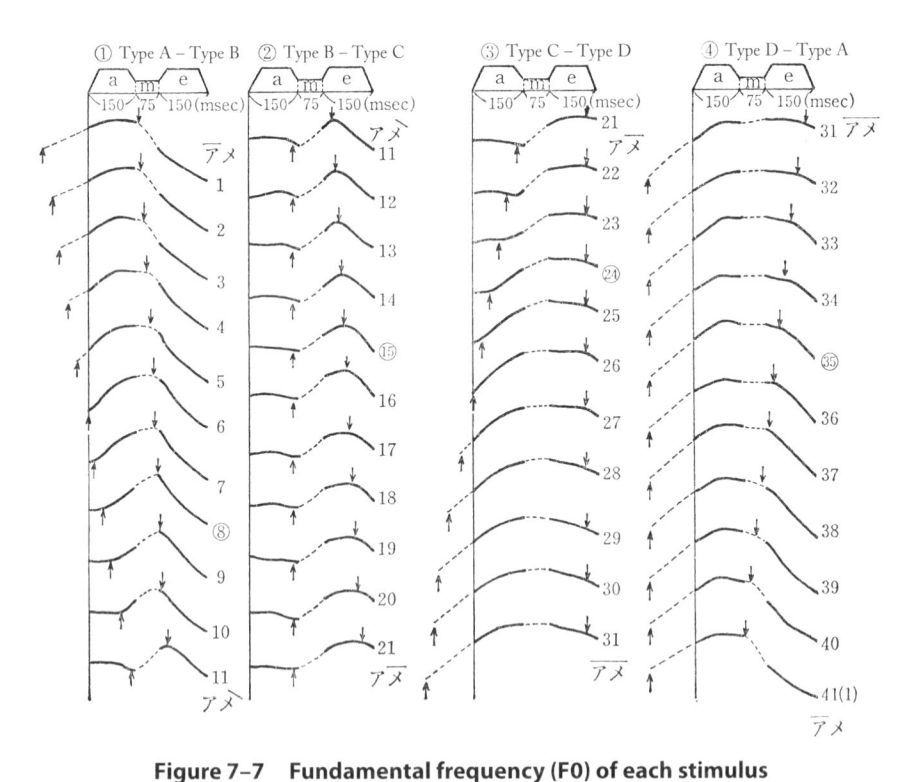

Figure 7-7　Fundamental frequency (F0) of each stimulus

F0 contour (pitch contour) of sound stimuli (1) No. 1 – No. 11, (2) No. 11 – No. 21, (3) No. 21 – No. 31, (4) No. 31 – No. 1. (↑ indicates beginning and indicates ending points of accent command)↓

No.11, ② in No.11 – No.21, ③ in No.21 – No.31, and ④ in No.31 – No.1.

A perceptual experiment was carried out on the discriminations of stimuli in the four columns: /Type A – Type B/, /Type B – Type C/, /Type C – Type D/, and /Type D – Type A/. There were a total of four participants: three Kansai dialect speakers and one Tokyo dialect speaker.

Circled numbers in Figure 7–7 show the contour boundaries of the two accent types. The points that determine the boundaries between other accent types are ⑧ in the first column, ⑮ in the second column, ㉔ in the third column, and ㉟ in the fourth column. These will be called the "judgment boundary" of accent types.

This is how the 40 synthesized pitch contours were created. Next, four perceptual experiments were carried out on how these pitch contours are categorized into four accent types.

7–3 pérmit – permít as produced by the accent production model

In <Experiment 1>, increased intensity was observed.

In order to investigate whether intensity is what determines accent, the intensity of the original sounds was increased four times, and we observed how perception changed across each boundary. As a result, we found no change in accent perception <perception of accent type> even when the intensity of the sound was four times larger. This means that intensity cannot be said to have an influence on the perception of Japanese accent.

Next, <Experiment 2> investigated the relation between vowel duration and the point in time when the pitch was lowered.

Figure 7–8 shows the results of Experiment 2. Experiment ①-1 which has both the same pitch contour as ① Type A – Type B experiment as well as the same amount of changes in duration, pitch contours in ①-3 (dotted line shows consonant /m/), and the judgment boundary of accent is shifted.

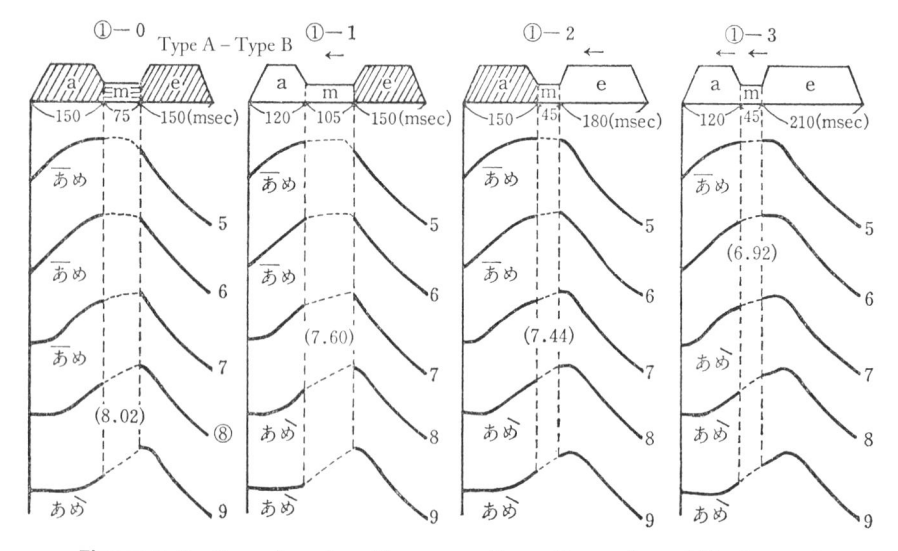

Figure 7–8 Experiment on the perception of boundary shift of accent
Pitch contours of Experiments ①-1, ①-3 that changes the durations of each sound and has the same pitch contours as A type – B type Experiment (dotted lines show the consonant /m/), and the movement of accent judgment threshold.

The perception of accent changes when the ratio of the consonant and vowel duration varies, keeping the duration of the whole word constant. Such an experiment can be done with synthesized sounds.

①-1, 2 in Figure 7–8 the sounds [m] and [e] are shifted to the front without changing the duration. The judgment boundary is shifted from 8.02 to 7.60, if you compare it with ①-0.

If [am] is shortened and [e] is expanded, as in ①-3, the accent boundary shifts from 6.92 to the dotted line. This means that the perception of accent changes when the timing of the rise and fall of pitch changes, thus changing which sound in a-m-e has a high pitch.

These experiments showed that the traditional way of thinking that accent cannot be detected unless intensity is considered is incorrect.

The next experiment, <Experiment 3>, is a perceptual experiment about English accent. The pitch contours of the pairs of two-syllable words pérmit – permít, and Japanese "ame" were compared. Figure 7–9 shows the pitch contour of English 'permit' compared with 11 synthesized Japanese 'ame'.

My interest in the changes in Type A from Type B, in other words, the changes in the pitch contours from the first 'ame' to the eleventh 'ame', started when I noticed the similarity of tone between Tokyo accent 'ame', Kansai accent 'ame', and English accent 'pérmit vs. permít'.

The changes above are regarded as the same as the changes of 'Ame' from 'a↓me'. Three American participants were presented with a judgment boundary test that had 11 synthesized versions of the English word 'permit', but the pitch contours were the same as those shown for the 11 pitch contours for 'ame' (No.1 to No.11).

The judgment boundary between 'pérmit' with an accent on the first syllable and 'permít' with an accent on the second syllable is the

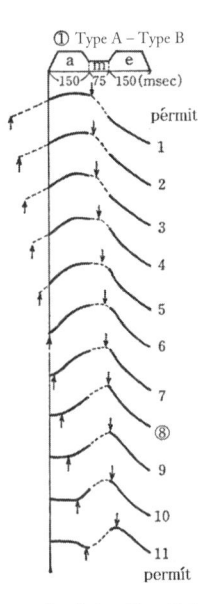

```
            ① Type A – Type B
              a  m  e
             150 75 150 (msec)
                    pérmit
                      1
                      2
                      3
                      4
                      5
                      6
                      7
                      ⑧
                      9
                      10
                      11
                    permít
```

Figure 7–9 Sound of the English word "permit".
The contours that show the changes in pitch of "voice" are 11 synthesized sounds ranging from "Ame" to "aME".

⑧ contour in Figure 7–9, the same as the judgment boundary in 'Ame – a↓me'.

7–4 Perceptual experiment with no-accent type speakers in six cities

The research started off with the purpose of investigating what an accent is. As I created synthesized stimuli for perceptual experiments and carried them out in various dialect regions, I came to think that these materials might make good educational materials for teaching accent.

The 40 synthesized stimuli were used to create four perceptual experiments (1) A – B, (2) B – C, (3) C – D, and (4) D – C.

Each experiment consisted of 10 randomized stimuli. The stimuli created for the perceptual experiments were made with the help of Professor Fujisaki and his laboratory members of the Department of Engineering at University of Tokyo.

First we performed a preliminary experiment with high school students nearby in Higashi Osaka, to make sure that the students participated with interest, and then we traveled from Tohoku to Kyushu to perform the experiment in various regions of Japan.

Specifically, the experiment was carried out at high schools in Yonezawa, Tokyo, Osaka, Fukui, Okayama, and Nagasaki, each having a different dialect.

We received permission and cooperation from the Principal of each school, and spent one hour to carry out the perceptual experiment in a sophomore class in each school (please refer to the accent map in Figure 4–1 for the locations of the high schools).

The accent types in each region may be summarized as below. Again, 'no accent region' refers to the regions where accent do not distinguish meanings in words.

(1) Tokyo accent region = Tokyo prefecture, Okayama city
(2) Kansai accent region (region with four accent types) = Osaka city
(3) Type 2 accent region (region with two accent types) = Nagasaki city
(4) No accent region = Yonezawa city, Fukui city

Japanese dialectal accent will be categorized into different accent regions when they are grouped by regions. A perceptual experiment was carried out at high schools in each region using synthesized sounds of four accent types. Figure 7–10 shows the results. Participants that did not have consistency in their judgment in the experiment of four accent types are shown with diagonal lines.

As the figure shows, in general, accent perception is influenced by individual differences as well as by regional differences.

There are differences in perception between the no-accent regions and the other regions. Additionally, there were differences in judgments of listeners in the Tokyo accent region and those in the Kansai accent region.

The next experiment is on the relation of accent type and musical

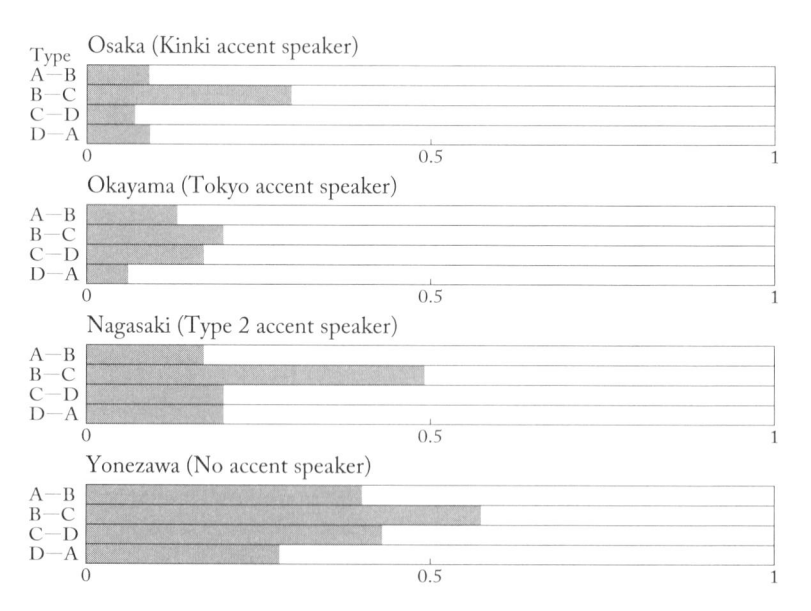

Figure 7–10 Numbers of people in each dialect that had mixed judgements in the four perceptual experiments

perception, and students of the university of music in Osaka participated as well. The results are shown in Figure 7-11.

The regions where the experiment was conducted with high school students are ● Osaka, ■ Tokyo, □ Okayama, + Nagasaki, ▲ Yonezawa, and △ Fukui, and the ○ mark shows the results from the 20 students majoring in music in Osaka.

The results showed that accent perception is related to musical perception. However, musical perception is not related to accurately producing accent types.

There was a case of a child with an accurate and stable dialectal accent who was influenced by his grandmother's dialectal accent. There are many interesting factors involved in accent production and

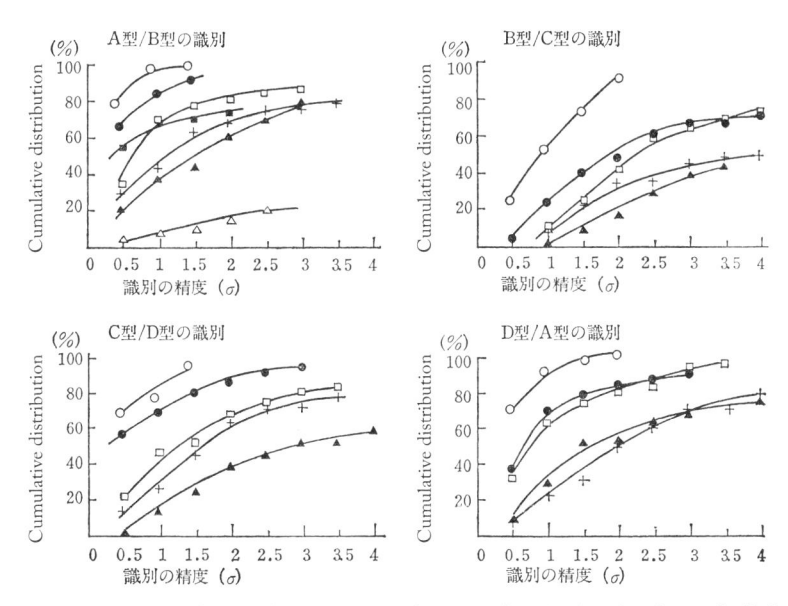

Figure 7-11 Cumulative distribution of accent discrimination in each dialect
High school students in ● Osaka, ■ Tokyo, □ Okayama, + Nagasaki, ▲ Yonezawa, and △ Fukui. ○: University students in Osaka majoring in music.

perception.

Next, a 45-minute class of what accent is was given to high school students in Fukui, a no-accent type region. After understanding what accent is, the same perception experiment was given to the students. The outcome showed that students in no-accent regions are clearly able to score higher scores in accent perception after receiving some accent training.

I learned a lot of things through observing that high school students enthusiastically and willingly participate in the experiments. I realized that education needs the system and tactics to enhance learners' curiosity and enthusiasm. I would like to thank the school principals and teachers for their enthusiastic cooperation, and the students for showing interest in the experiments.

These results showed that Japanese accent is judged by pitch, and not by intensity. Moreover, it became clear that pitch determines the accent production and perception even in the case of English. The next chapter will be on experiments concerning phoniatrics.

CHAPTER 8:

Accent commands from the brain —— electromyography

> The experimental results up to here have shown that English accent, traditionally thought to be a stress accent, was actually judged by pitch, similar to Japanese.
>
> With the help of the phoniatric examinations, I wished to observe this point using physiological methods. But before getting into that, we must still solve the problem of Kansai accent, which has a falling accent.
>
> First, features of accent production in Kansai accent will be observed, and then we will look into the electromyography of English productions.

8-1 What is electromyography?

Professor Shiro Hattori in the Language Department at the University of Tokyo suggested carrying out experiments at the Phonetics Laboratory in the Medical Department at University of Tokyo. The Phonetics Laboratory was a logopedics and phoniatrics research institute in the field of cognitive logopedics in the Medical

Department. Professor Hattori had always academically collided with Professor Izui, filling the conference at the Linguistics Society with tension, which was an excellent occasion to do research. Professor Hattori was especially strict to me, being a follower of Professor Izui, so the offer was unexpected. I was, however, grateful to be able to participate in physiological experiments.

Professor Hajime Hirose called out to me by name on the corridor of the Phonetics Laboratory at the Medical Department at University of Tokyo. He was an expert on research concerning laryngeal electromyography. Due to meeting for the first time on that spot, I was able to conduct a joint research on recording the laryngeal electromyography of Kansai dialect speakers. I am originally from Tokyo, so unfortunately could not participate as the Kansai accent speaker. Luckily, a female assistant YI of my laboratory had confidence in using Kansai accent, and was enthusiastic about taking part in the experiment. I took the assistant to the Phonetics Laboratory twice. There were other applicants as well, and two of them participated.

First, electromyography of each laryngeal muscle is recorded with a multi-channel FM data recorder along with sound signals.

Figure 8–1 shows the positions of the Lateral Cricoarytenoid (LCA), Cricothyroid (CT), and Sternohyoid (SH) (Hirose, Simada and Ohala, 1969). The LCA has a function of closing the glottis. CT has a function of producing a high-pitched voice. The SH in those days was not known for sure whether it functioned in lowering the pitch of the voice, although it is known to function in lowering the jaw.

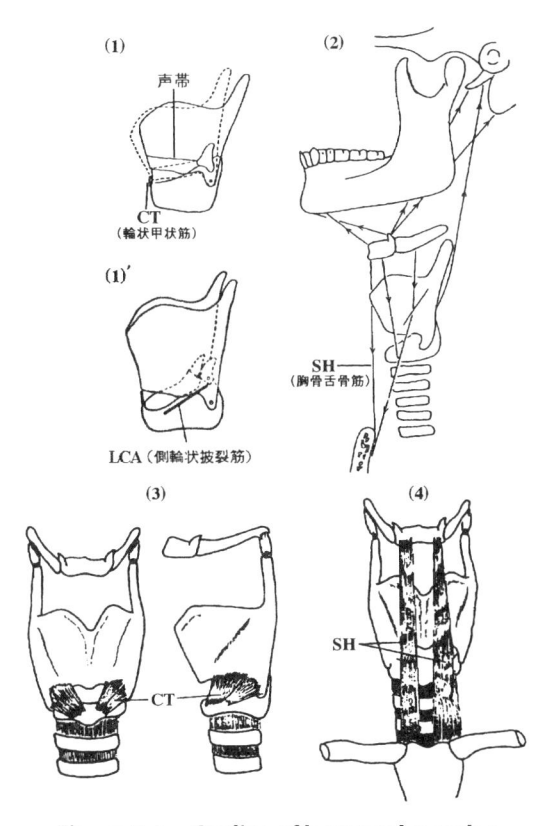

Figure 8-1　Outline of laryngeal muscles
(1) Thyroid cartilage (where there is vocal folds inside)
(2) Thyroid cartilage and its surroundings
(3) Cricothyroid (CT) from front and side
(4) Sternohyoid (SH) from front (reference: Zemlin 1968)

The following is a summary of the function of each muscle.

LCA is a muscle that functions when the glottis closes, so it has a relation with the nerve command when producing voicing.

CT is related to the adjustment of voice pitch. When this muscle contracts, the vocal folds are pulled back, and the tension of the vocal folds increase.

SH is related to the lowering of the voice pitch, as well as activities of opening the jaw, lowering the tongue, and moving the tongue backwards. In order to lower the voice pitch, it is important for the tension of CT to decrease. However, the involvement of SH has been controversial.

Electromyography is usually processed by computers by averaging over a number of (12 times) repetitions. However, it is difficult to see the actual muscle activity. Therefore Figure 8–2 shows the raw data from electromyography (Sugito and Hirose, 1978).

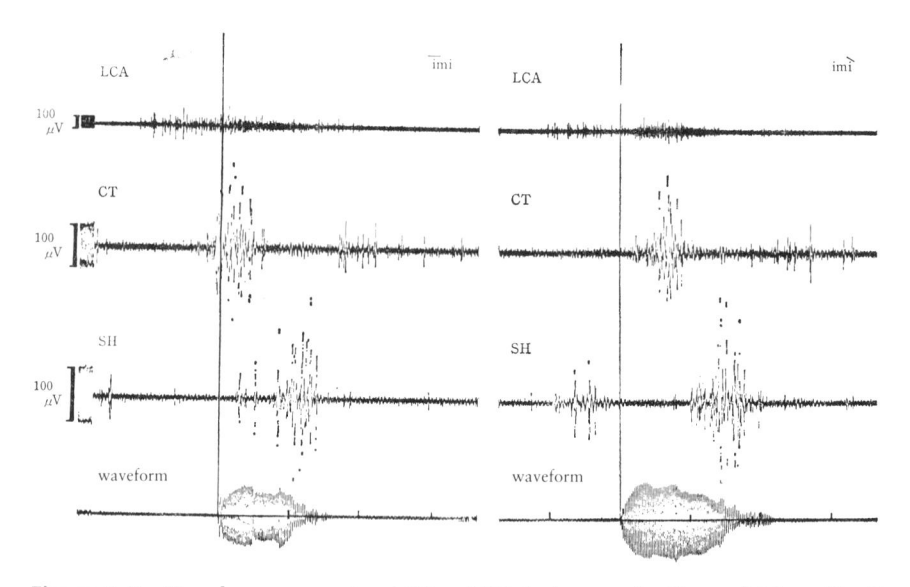

Figure 8–2   Muscle movements of CT and SH during productions of A type "Imi" and B type "i↓mi" (Subject Y.I.)

8-2 Muscle activity features recorded from electromyography when speaking with Kansai dialect

Figure 8–2 shows the production of 'Imi' and 'i↓mi' recorded in each channel with an FM data recorder. The action potentials of each muscle were displayed on the recording paper using a photo recorder. The technician was Mr. Imagawa. The action potentials of LCA, CT, and SH are shown from the top down respectively, and the bottom shows the sound waves. The solid vertical line shows the beginning of the sound wave, which refers to the 0 point in time; the x-axis shows the duration of the sound.

The scale of 100 µV (micro volts) on the left side of the figure shows the amplitude for each muscle activity. The action potentials of each muscle during production of HL type with a high start are shown in the left figure, and LHL type with a low start are shown in the right figure. The speaker is the Kansai dialect speaker, YI.

Vocal folds are widely open in order to breathe, but the glottis (where the vocal folds are) closes in an instant when we produce voice. When producing sounds with an accent, the vocal folds become tense and elongated in order to increase the pitch. In preparation, the LCA becomes active.

Next, the brain sends a command to the CT to increase the pitch. This makes the vocal folds elongate and produce voice with high pitch. During the EMG experiments, a needle which holds a wire thinner than a hair is inserted into the CT and SH.

The CT and SH activities are first amplified. By recording these data, we can see the activation of the muscles, as in Figure 8-2. When raising the pitch, the CT becomes active. The activity in the CT is what makes the voice rise in the case of Tokyo accent according to earlier research, but this was the first experiment carried out on Kansai accent.

The relation with the rise and fall of voice in SH had especially been unclear, although it is clearly related to the lowering of the jaw. If you raise your chin and touch around the throat, there are two long muscles on either side of your throat that you can feel. These are the SH (sternohyoid) muscles that connect the jaw and the sternum. How does this come to relate with voice pitch? The fact that SH contracts when you open your mouth and lower your jaw was clear, but whether SH muscles were involved in the rise and fall of voice pitch was unclear at that time.

Hereafter, the laryngeal electromyography will show the results of averages of 12 repetitions of the same words.

8-3　How about 'electromyography' when speaking in English?

Let's look at the experimental examples of English words 'pérmit' and 'permít'. This electromyography was obtained at Haskins Laboratory in the United States (Hirose and Sawashima, 1979).

We asked English native speakers to be participants in the

electromyographic experiment. The purpose was to confirm that English word accent involved changes in voice pitch.

Figure 8–3 (1) shows the results. In several of the electromyographic data, the action potentials for the laryngeal muscle CT of the two productions 'pérmit' and 'permít' are shown. They are the averages of the 12 repetitions.

Figure 8–3 (2) shows the laryngeal electromyography (CT) (top), SH (middle) and pitch contours (bottom) during productions of 'Imi'(HL) and 'im↓i' (LHL). They are the averages of the electromyography of 12 repetitions by Kansai dialect speaker YI.

CT activation before the rise in the voice pitch and relaxation of CT before lowering the voice pitch are observed in the case of English 'pérmit – permít' in the same manner as the case of Japanese 'imi – imi'. This figure clearly shows that the differences in the two English accents are accompanied by a rise and lowering of voice pitch due to CT activation.

Figure 8–3 (3) shows the laryngeal electromyography (top) and the pitch contours (bottom) of five words "india, indigenous, individual, individuality, individualization". The accented syllables are each shifted one syllable toward the end in the above words.

In all of the words, CT activation of voice pitch rising is observed approximately 0.1 seconds before accented syllables. This show that the neural on/off commands for pitch rising activates the CT, resulting in changes in voice pitch which creates the perceived lexical accent.

As previously stated, the activation of SH preceding voice pitch fall has been controversial. It is merely a hypothesis, but in the case of

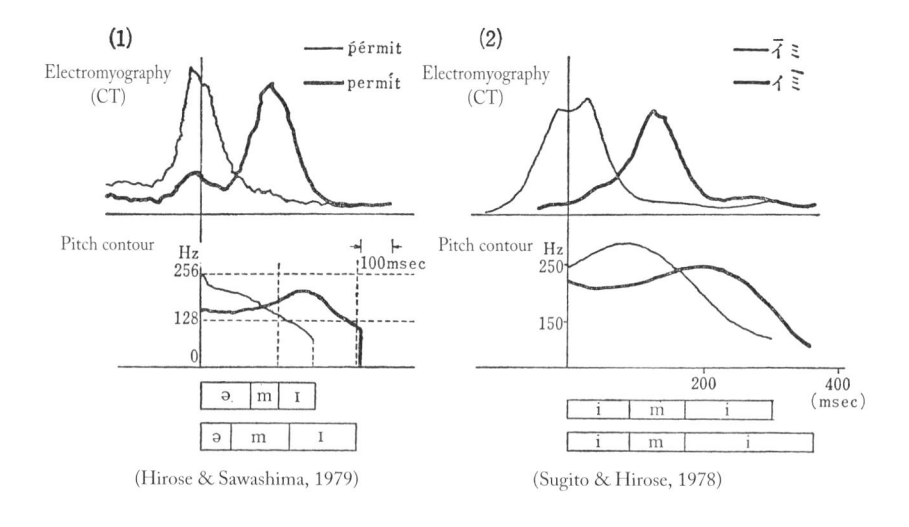

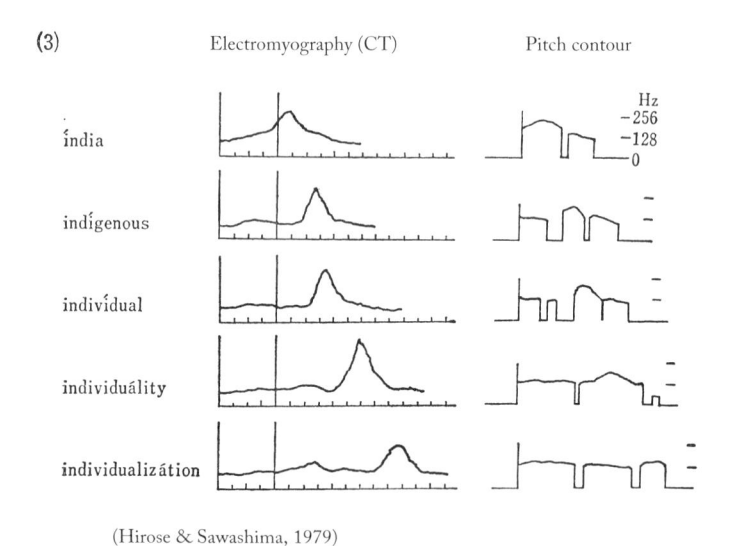

Figure 8–3 Laryngeal electromyogram and pitch contours of (1) pérmit / permít, (2) Imi / i↓mi, and (3) five English words

Laryngeal electromyogram (top) and pitch contours (bottom) of (1) pérmit and permít, and (2) "Imi" and "i↓mi". (3) shows the laryngeal electromyogram (top) and pitch contours (bottom) of the five words whose accent shifts one syllable towards the end of the word.

English, SH is not necessarily activated during word accent production. In the Kinki dialect, SH, as Figure 8–2 shows, is activated when the pitch on the vowel is shifted rapidly from high to low, and when the final part is even more lowered, or when the voice pitch is low at the beginning. In the case of English, SH may be used to bring about the pitch fall especially in emphatic expressions along with relaxation of the CT.

Additionally, there is a study that discusses the relation between the activation of laryngeal muscle and pitch fall during voice pitch changes in English accent production. The laryngeal electromyography such as CT and SH as well as subglottal pressure were measured in the study, and the relation between fundamental frequency was discussed. The voice pitch for the emphasized word in the three declarative and three question utterances of "Bev loves Bob, (i.e., BEV loves Bob; Bev LOVES Bob; Bev loves BOB; BEV loves Bob?; Bev LOVES Bob?; and Bev loves BOB?") is positively related to CT, as well as subglottal pressure, and also has a negative relation with SH. It seems that the argument that SH activation is related to low pitch is especially worth paying attention to.

If you look at the data (e.g., 8–2), we can clearly see what the SH is doing. It has been questioned whether SH activity is related to the rising and falling of voice pitch. However, we know that the brain must send a command to the muscle before the changes in voice pitch are produced as in the cases of-both at the beginning of the low-starting word and at the end of the word with falling pitch, as in the example of Kansai accent "ame"(LHL)". Please note, in both situations of low pitch, similar movements of SH are observed.

8–4 EMG productions of [a] and [i] are different

In the previous chapters I discussed the acoustic characteristics of Kansai dialect speakers productions of /imi/ with four accent types. Why did I choose the word /imi/ and not /ame/?

The reason is that the data may be influenced by the lowering of the jaw in the productions of /a/, /e/, and /o/. Using a high vowel /i/ is effective in order to avoid such influence.

Figure 8–4 shows the function of SH at the beginning of a low-pitch type word. For the LHL type, where beginning is low, then high, and then the voice is lowered, SH is functioning before for both of the lowering of the voice. Types A to D in Figure 8–4 show, from the top to bottom, the pitch contour, CT, SH, and the sound amplitude. The productions are by a Kansai dialect speaker, YI.

The experiment conducted in 1972 showed that the productions of Kansai accent are essentially different from that of the Tokyo dialect. With this result, I understood why I could not imitate the sentence intonation of "ame futtekita (it started to rain)" immediately after moving to Kansai. The physiological features during production are different.

Minoru Wada (1947) proposed the distinction of two types of accent: low-beginning and high-beginning in Kansai accent, and the experimental results obtained here belatedly provided supportive

CHAPTER 8: Accent commands from the brain

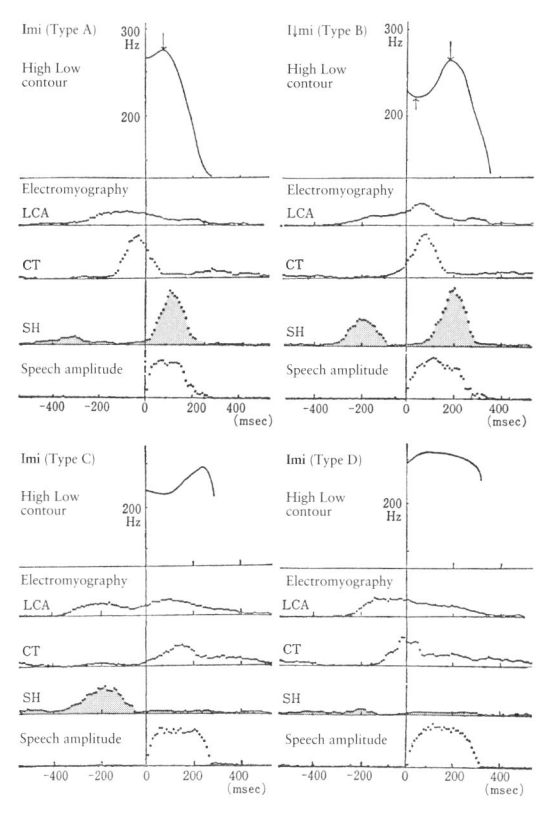

Figure 8–4 Laryngeal electromyogram during accent type productions
Four accent types (Types A, B, C, and D) of [imi]. (From top: pitch contour, CT, SH, and amplitude) (subject Y.I.)

evidence.

I was told not to present the results of the SH function at conferences. I guess it was because it was questioned that the SH function was greatly different from that of the Tokyo accent despite being the same language. Or, it may have been because the results do not correspond with the previously published "Production model of Japanese accent".

8–5   The reason I wanted English 'electromyography'

Right about that time, two professors of the Phonetics Laboratory at the University of Tokyo were going to visit a laboratory in the United States. I asked them to get the laryngeal electromyography of English word productions including 'pérmit – permít', and they kindly accepted. The results are shown in Figure 8–3 (3). I was able to receive the data three years later.

The results showed CT activation preceding the rise in pitch for producing lexical accent, similar to what had been observed for Japanese. It is a pity that the SH experiment was not done also.

Thanks to the laryngeal electromyography, we were able to understand to a certain extent how the laryngeal muscles worked to produce pitch changes in the Kansai accent, and also, the physiological differences in the production of accent in the Kansai and Tokyo dialects.

Kansai accent differs from Tokyo starting right from the production stage; the SH used for lowering the pitch of the voice is used in the Kansai dialect but not in the Tokyo one. This discovery provided supportive evidence that Kansai accent distinguishes the two types of accents: low-starting and high-starting.

Additionally, it also proved that English word accent is created from laryngeal muscles that control voice pitch, in opposition to the widely accepted theory that English word accent is mostly stress-related. It also corresponded well with the acoustical experimental results that I had long been conducting research on.

It has long been considered that "The origin of the regional dialectal accents across Japan is Kansai, and it gradually changed into something different", but these experimental results also proved that this was not the case.

The Research Institute of Logopedics and Phoniatrics at the University of Tokyo is closed. I participated in research when the institute had been active, and was able to obtain valuable experimental material concerning accent production. I'd like to express my sincere gratitude to Professor Sawashima and Professor Hirose and to the technical staff, Mr. Hiroshi Imagawa.

CHAPTER 9:

Observing the 'accent command' from the brain

> Accented voiceless mora, along with 'late pitch fall', have been regarded as evidence that Japanese accent is not really pitch accented. It is illogical to say that accent kernels exist in mora with no vocal fold vibration. But if accented voiceless mora actually exist, we therefore must investigate what physiological activity happens during the voiceless vowel. In this chapter, I explain the results of phoniatric examinations in which I dared to challenge the experiments that are generally thought to be impossible.

9–1 Combination of 'mora sound' and 'voice pitch'

Since there is no vocal fold vibration in voiceless mora, no voice pitch can exist for that mora. However, actually, there are some instances in which the pitch of the following vowel, with a slight delay, is high in the beginning and falling at the end. This is caused by a command from the brain to produce accent. As I said earlier, the pitch of the mora before the falling pitch is high. So this phenomenon agrees with my earlier explanation that the mora following the accented high mora has falling pitch.

Let's try to examine if we can observe the kind of electromyographic (EMG) command from the brain to raise the voice pitch in the voiceless mora, even though there is no vocal fold vibration during the vowel portion of the mora.

Figure 9–1 shows the overlaid pitch contours from 12 productions each of two speakers (MM on the top, YI on the bottom) recorded simultaneously with the EMG recordings. The two figures ① and ③ on the left are 'kusa (grass)', and the two figures ② and ④ on the right are 'kusi (comb)'. The starting points of the second vowels for each of the twelve productions are shown at the vertical axis, and the lowering of the voice is shown with '▼'.

The two 'kusi' figures ② and ④ on the right look similar; however, these kusi figures and the kusa figures ① and ③ on the left are quite different. The individual /kusa/ productions by speaker MM on the top clearly show 12 different productions but the /kusa/ productions by speaker YI at the bottom show only one instance of a pitch contour for the /u/ (vowel on the first mora /ku/) on the left. This is because voicing is present on the first mora only once out of the twelve productions by speaker YI, and for the other 11 productions, the vowels are all devoiced.

Notice that the pronunciation of 'kusi' is actually "kushi" in Japanese, but is written in the Japanese phonological system as "kusi".

CHAPTER 9: Observing the 'accent command' from the brain 111

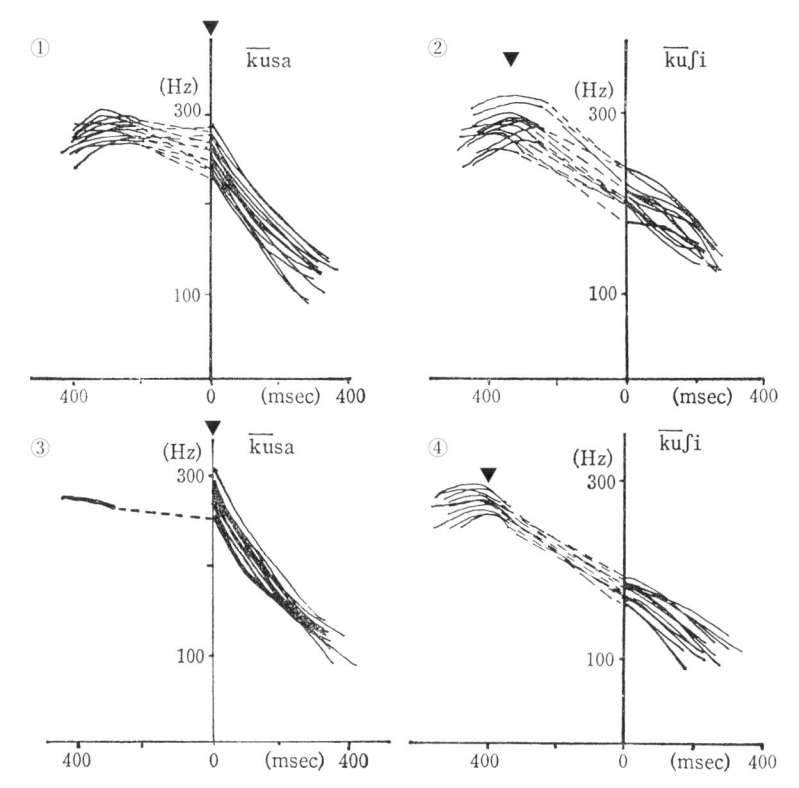

Figure 9-1 **Twelve pitch contours of two speakers (top: subject MM, bottom: subject YI) while extracting laryngeal electromyogram.**
Figures ① and ③: "KUsa" ('grass'). Figures ② and ④: "KUsi" ('comb') Fall in the pitch is indicated with the symbol ▼.

Thus the pronunciation of the s-sound in 'grass' ('kusa') is an s-sound, and that in 'comb' ('kusi') is an sh-sound. In phonetics the s-sound is usually written as [s] and the sh-sound as [ʃ]. However, there is no significant difference in the durations of [s] and [ʃ] in the total of 24 productions of [kusa] and [kuʃi] by speaker YI.

Next, the vowels on the second mora in kusi and kusa are different (/i/ and /a/), and you will also see that the pitch contours are quite different when you compare the figures on the left and right.

The '▼' in the figure show the timing where the voice pitch starts to drop. The timing for kusi on the right figure is at the end of the vowel in 'ku', in other words, just before the 's' (dashed line). The timing of the pitch fall for kusa in the left figure, on the other hand, is delayed and occurs after the 's', or at the beginning of the second vowel 'a'. Thus, the timing of voice pitch fall in 'kusa' is considerably delayed compared to [kuʃi].

Let's observe the laryngeal electromyography that we looked at in Chapter 8, and see how voice pitch is raised and lowered, and the timing of it relative to the production of the mora.

9–2 The answer to the puzzle —— matching the timing of 'sound of the mora' to the 'voice pitch'

Produced with the Kansai accent, 'kushi (comb)' and 'kusa (grass), the timing of to lower the voice pitch (starting point of fall voice pitch) is at the end of [ku] for [kuʃi], and at the beginning of [s]. As for the production of [kusa], however, the timing of pitch falling is delayed and is after the [s], or at the beginning of [a]. Why does this (delay) happen?

As mentioned in the previous chapter, the articulatory movements for lowering the voice pitch and lowering the jaw for producing the sound [a] can be carried out simultaneously due to the function of the SH (sternohyoid). The timing of the command for lowering the voice pitch may be matched with the opening of the jaw for producing [a].

CHAPTER 9: Observing the 'accent command' from the brain

In such cases, the lowering of the voice pitch is delayed, and the lowering of the jaw during the production of [a] may be carried out at the same time by using SH.

For example, in figure 9–1, the lowering of the voice pitch (indicated with a black arrow) is at the end of the first mora [ku] and at the beginning of the second mora [ʃi]. There is no problem because the first mora is high, and the second mora is low.

In the case of 'kusa (grass)', on the other hand, there is no change in pitch until the end of [ku], but as the [s] in the second mora [sa] shifts to the following vowel [a], the pitch rapidly descends from high to low for both speakers. The point at which the voice pitch descends due to accent and that for producing the vowel [a] by lowering the jaw completely matches. That is, the voice pitch begins to descend at the beginning of [a].

Figure 9–2 is the answer to the question why the beginning of [a] and the timing of voice pitch descending occur simultaneously. The figures show the productions of (a) kusi, (b) kusa, and (c) kusa, from top to bottom. The figures (a), (b), and (c) on the left are measurements of spectrograms, and show the changes over time in the voice pitch. The figures on the right show the sound amplitude and laryngeal electromyography of CT (cricothyroid), and the activity of SH (bottom).

Please notice that the first mora in (c) kusa is devoiced, and we can clearly see CT activation for raising pitch as also is seen in the case of (b) kusa.

Chapter 8 mentioned that the CT becomes active in order to raise

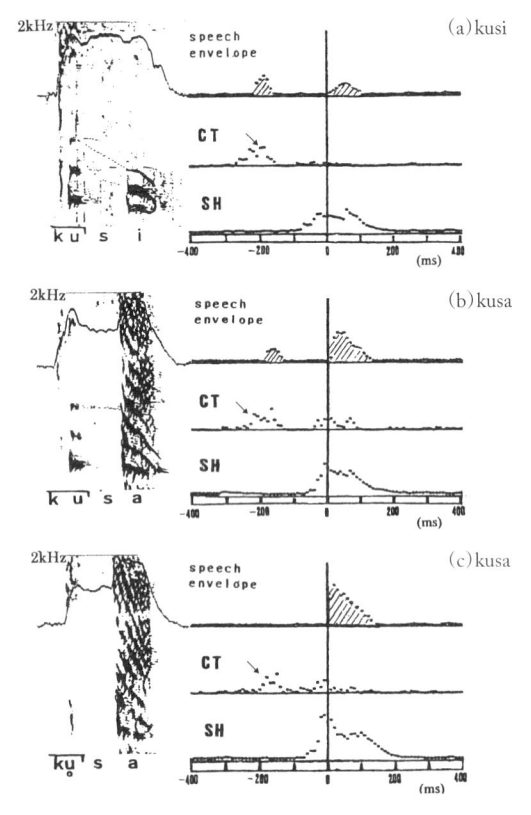

Figure 9-2 Voiceless mora and laryngeal electromyography
From top: (a) kusi (b) kusa and (c) kusa (example of devoiced first mora)
The figures on the left, all (a) (b) and (c) are spectrograms that show durational changes in pitch).
The figures on the right, all (a) (b) and (c), show at the top, amplitude and laryngeal electromyogram, and at the bottom: SH movements.

Note: Out of the three productions, the first vowel in (c) kusa, is devoiced. However, as in the case of voiced vowel in (b) kusa, we can observe clear CT activity to raise the pitch.

the voice pitch, but SH becomes active when lowering the voice pitch. The following is a summary of it once again.

The beginning of the second vowel [a] in [kusa] is delayed compared to the beginning of the second vowel [i] in [kuʃi]. By using

SH, lowering the jaw for producing [a] and lowering the voice pitch must be performed simultaneously. The way the brain uses time and energy is economical, and it is of a great surprise that the timing matches precisely.

The human brain has an organized, disciplined, and calculated function. Otherwise, the human hand would not be able to perform delicate work using fingers, or pianists, for example, performing fascinating pieces of music by controlling melody with the right hand and rhythm with the left.

9–3   I got it! —— Both Japanese and English have pitch accents!

In the West, it was generally believed that the English word accent was called a stress, and stress was based on the intensity or duration (Fry, 1955).

However, Bolinger (1958) came to the conclusion that English accent is based on pitch. The experiment using re-synthesized sounds where the vowels in each syllable were intensified and changed into a higher pitch in the sentence 'Break both apart' concluded that pitch is more effective than intensity in accent perception. According to Bolinger, the factor that emphasizes accented syllables in a sentence is the prominence of pitch, and with some extra duration and intensity, accent if formed. At present, pitch is the main condition considered in synthesized English sounds.

I performed research on the dynamics of voice pitch by investigating and comparing the measurements of all sound waves and the changes in the fundamental frequency of 550 words in each of the two major dialects of Japanese (Tokyo accent and Kansai accent), which was thought to be a pitch accent, and 400 words in English. As a result, English word accent was based on the dynamic changes in the voice pitch, just as in Japanese (Sugito, 1980, 1982). As Bolinger claimed above, 'English accent is formed with the prominence of pitch, with some extra duration and intensity'. There are similarities with my experiment, but the quality and scale are much smaller. In addition to the bigger scale in the experiment I did, pitch is the only condition necessary. Japanese and English are clearly languages with pitch accents. This is the result that I verified though many long years of acoustic-phonetic, psychological and phoniatric experiments.

CHAPTER 10:

What is the difference between English and Japanese accent?

> It has long been believed that English word accent is based on intensity. However, the experiments have shown that English accent is actually based on the changes of voice pitch. This was proved with the results of physiological experiments during productions as well.
>
> This chapter will introduce an experiment that analyzed the Aesop's Fables spoken by English and Japanese native speakers. Please notice that the function of accent in Japanese and English are greatly different. Additionally, the narration of the story 'Momotaro' in Japanese, along with the translated English version, will also be explained in order to show the characteristics of reading by Japanese speakers.

10–1 English and Japanese accent, and the characteristics of narration

The basic unit of Japanese accent is a mora, as introduced in Chapter 2. The basic unit for English accent, on the other hand, is a syllable. Moreover, a vowel is not limited to one. There are diphthongs and even three-vowel clusters. There are also cases where more than two consonants precede or follow these vowels. They form a syllable.

The differences of Japanese and English accent, and the ways the native speakers speak, are summarized as follows.

(A) Japanese accent
- High-low pitch in each word accent is always expressed in spoken speech.
- → Accent is used to distinguish the meanings of each word.

(B) English accent
- Accent in each word is not always expressed in spoken speech.
- Words the speaker wants to emphasize are produced clearly with a high pitch on the accented syllable.
- → The main points of the story are clearly conveyed.

(A') The way Japanese speakers speak
- When they start reading, the pitch tends to become higher.
- The pitch rises and falls within a sentence in order to express accent in each word.
- → It is not clear to the listener where the speaker wants to emphasize.

(B') The way English speakers speak
- Normally, they begin to speak with a low, comfortable pitch.

- Each word accent is not expressed in sentences.
- Emphasis is on the accented syllables on words that are important to the speaker. The syllable, as a result, has a high pitch.
→ It is easier for the listener to comprehend, because the speaker emphasizes the parts that he wants to convey.

10-2 Comparison of Japanese and English narrations

The experimental material used here is a short Aesop's Fable. English native speakers read it in English, and the Japanese native speakers read it in Japanese. The following passages were given to the speakers.

【English】
　Everyman carries two bags about with him. One in front, one behind, and both are full of faults. The bag in front contains his neighbor's faults, and the one behind his own. Therefore men do not see their own faults, but never fail to see those of others.

【Japanese】
　人は誰でもいつも２つの袋を下げています。ひとつは前に、ひとつは後ろに。２つとも、過ちがいっぱい入っています。前の袋には身近な人の過ちが、後ろの袋には自分の過ちが入っています。それで、人は、自分の過ちには気付かないで、目の前に見える他の人

の過ちは決して見のがすことがないのです。

The passage in (1) shows the Tokyo accent, and (2) shows the Kansai accent. The line above the words show the accent position in each word, and Japanese native speakers read those parts with a high pitch. However, when meanings are adjacent as in 'fuTATSUnofukuro' and 'hiTOtsuhamaeni' in Tokyo accent, the latter may not be produced with a high pitch.

(1) Example of Tokyo accent (with word accent)
hiTOHADAredemo Itumo **fuTATSUnofuKURO**woMOtteimasu. hi TOtsuhaMAeni hiTOtsuhauSIRONISAgeteimasu. fuTATSUTOMOa YAMACHIgaiPPAIHAitteimasu. MAenofuKUROniha MIDIKANAHI TONOaYAMACHIga uSIRONOfuKUROnihajiBUNNOaYAMACHI gaHAitteimasu. soREDEhiTOHAjiBUNNOaYAMACHInihakiDUKA naide TAnohitonoaYAMACHIhakeSSITEmiNOGASUKOTOgaNAi nodesu.

(2) Example of Kansai accent
HItohadareDEmo iTSUmo FUTAtsunoDUkurowomotTEimasu. **HI TOtsuhamaEni** HITOtsuhaUsironisageteimaSU. futatsuTOMOAYA MACHIGAippaIhaitteImasu. maEnoFUkuroniha MIDIKAnaHItono AYAMACHIGA UsironoFUkuronihajibunnoAYAMACHIGAhaitteI masu. SOREDE HItohajibunnoAYAMACHINIhaKIDUKAnaide tano HItonoAYAMACHIHAkesSIteMINOGASUKOtoganaInodeSU.

The following experiment was conducted with 18 participants in order to investigate how accent expression is different in English spoken by English native speakers and English spoken by Japanese native speakers.

The participants were first grouped into (A) English speakers / English teachers, (B) Japanese speakers / English teachers, and (C) Japanese speakers / students. The place of birth is shown in parentheses. Japanese speakers are limited to Kansai dialect speakers.

(A) English speakers / English teachers: 6 participants (Americans; Nebraska, Wisconsin, Iowa, New York; Canadians; Montreal; British; Berkshire.) Please notice that they are all from different places.
(B) Japanese speakers / English teachers: 6 participants (Kansai)
(C) Japanese speakers / students: 6 participants (Kansai)

I had the participants read aloud the passage, and extracted the pitch. The English speakers showed very similar productions of accent, even though they were all from different places.

10–3 Which words are emphasized?

Among the pitch contours by the 18 participants, analysis especially focused on the accented high-pitched parts. The number of words with increased pitch was noted for each of the three groups.

Figure 10–1 shows the histogram of the six participants in (A) to (C) who produced a high pitch in the words on the left.

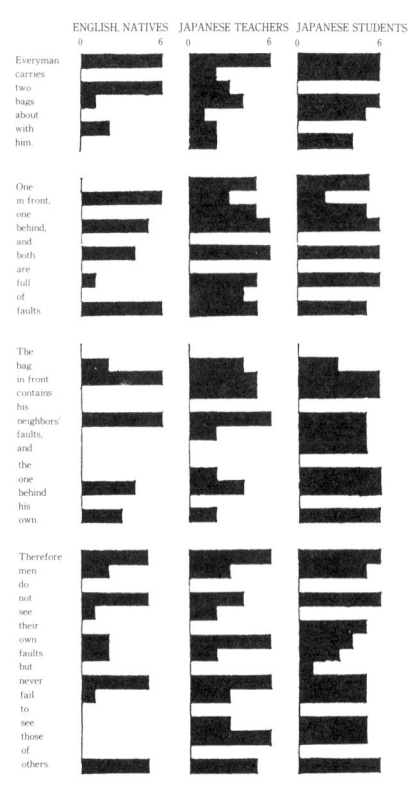

Figure 10-1 Histogram of the numbers of people that produced words at the left in high pitch. Speakers: (A) English natives, (B) Japanese teachers of English, (C) Japanese students

The groups are from left to right (A) English speakers, (B) Japanese speakers of English (teachers), and (C) Japanese speakers of English (students). Each occurrence of when a speaker produced a particular word (shown on the left of the graph) with a high pitch is indicated as a bar graph on the horizontal axis.

CHAPTER 10: What is the difference between English and Japanese accent?

As a result, the number of participants that produced a high pitch was small for (A), large for (C), and (B) was around the middle.

The words that five out of six or all of the participants produced with a high pitch were 'everyman, two, in front, faults, in front, neighbor's, therefore, not, never, others' (underlined). Please notice that these words function as key words in the story.

<u>Everyman</u> carries <u>two</u> bags about with him. One <u>in front</u>, one behind, and both are full of <u>faults</u>. The bag <u>in front</u> contains his <u>neighbor's</u> faults, and the one behind his own. <u>Therefore</u> men do <u>not</u> see their own faults, but <u>never</u> fail to see those of <u>others</u>.

In contrast, the productions of the students in Group (C) had emphasis on almost all of the words, and like Japanese, they are reading with a clear accent on each word.

In the case of English, the differences between Japanese and English speakers are of the following.

① two bags

In this story, the key is that there are two bags, one in front, and one in back. English speakers therefore emphasize 'two', but Japanese speakers emphasize 'bags'.

② one in front, one behind

English speakers emphasize the positions of the two bags 'front', but Japanese speakers emphasize 'one'. Additionally, English speakers produce 'behind' with a longer duration.

③ full of faults

This is the most important phrase. English speakers emphasize 'faults', but Japanese speakers emphasize both 'full' and 'faults', and have a tendency of emphasizing 'full' more. Additionally, 'faults' emerge in the story three times. Although English speakers emphasize only the first 'faults', Japanese speakers do not. They emphasize each time the word 'faults' occurs.

There are many challenges for Japanese speakers in learning to read and speak English. Generally, for Japanese speakers of English, there is no connection between what is emphasized and the content of the story. Instructions of reading aloud or speaking should be clearly spelled out, and particularly, it should be taught which words should be emphasized.

10–4　Which parts should have a high pitch?

Next, only the 'Everyman carries two bags about with him' part is extracted from the pitch contour, and we shall observe how English and Japanese speakers read them.

In the first sentence 'Everyman carries two bags about with him', all participants emphasized the first word 'Everyman'. This word is important because the word should convey the message that 'everyone',

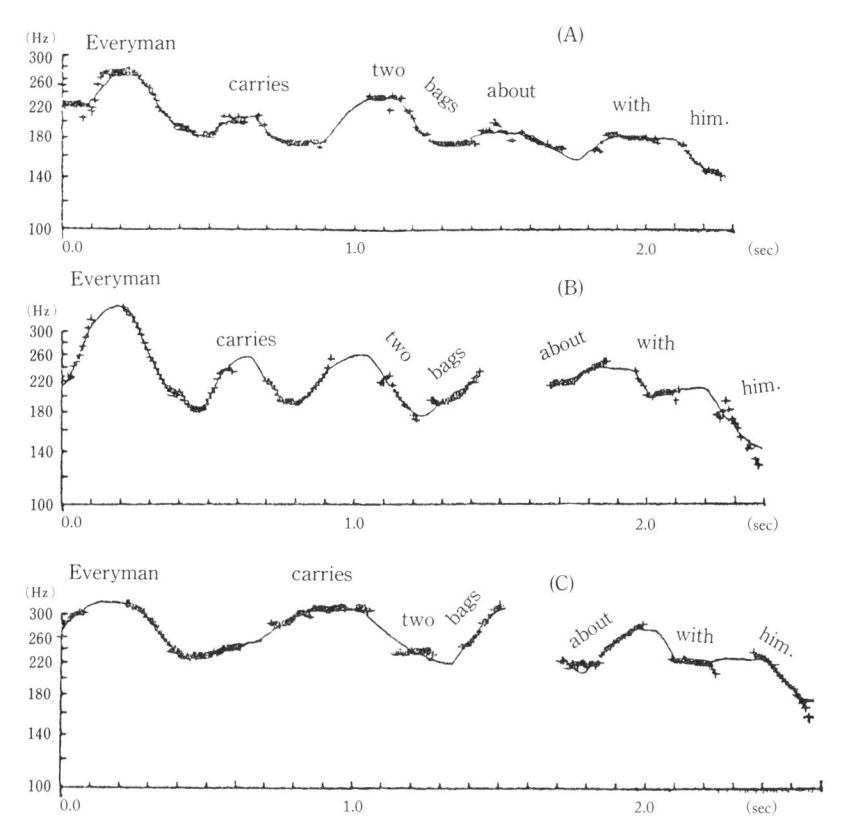

CHAPTER 10: What is the difference between English and Japanese accent? 125

Figure 10-2 Pitch contours of 'Everyman carries two bags about with him.'
(A) English natives, (B) Japanese speaker (English teacher), (C) Japanese speaker

with no exceptions, owns two bags.

Next, English speakers emphasizes 'two' in 'two bags', but Japanese speakers produce 'two' in a low pitch, and 'bag' in a high pitch. The fact that there are two bags is important in this story, therefore 'two' should be emphasized.

Figure 10–3 shows the pitch contour of the second sentence 'One in front, one behind, and both are full of faults'. The parts of voiceless consonants are substituted with a line, showing where the voiceless

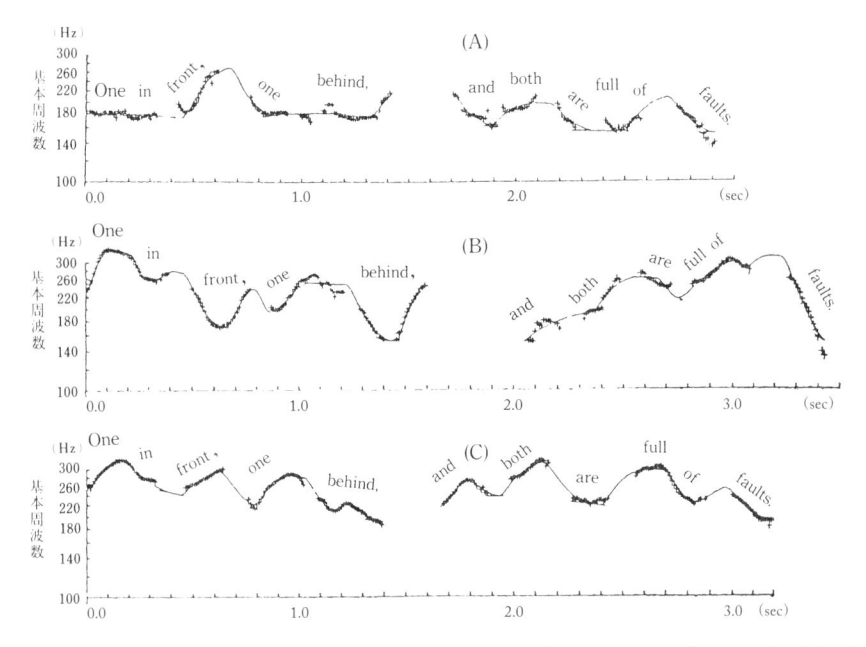

Figure 10-3 Pitch contours of 'One in front, one behind, and both are full of faults' (A) English natives, (B) Japanese speaker (English teacher), (C) Japanese speaker

consonants are.

English speakers emphasize 'in front' and 'behind' which are important words that indicate the positions of the bags, and produce 'one' in a low pitch. Japanese speakers produce 'one' in a high pitch, and put emphasis more on the word after the pause rather than on which word is important in terms of the meaning of the sentence. This makes the Japanese utterances of English sound flat.

The most important phrase in the story is 'full of faults'. English speakers emphasize 'faults', whereas Japanese speakers (teachers) emphasize 'full'. Japanese speakers (teachers) appropriately produce prepositions, articles, 'are', 'do' in a low pitch, but they did not focus on the importance of meaning. They also did not focus on the important phrases when reading the Japanese version of the passage.

English speakers put emphasis on important words in the sentence. Japanese speakers should learn this point, otherwise the English would not sound English-like, and will be difficult for the listeners to understand.

English learners should observe the figures, and try to match the changes of voice pitch with that of the English native speakers by reading out loud. You will notice the differences of producing accent between English and Japanese speakers' English if you try to read the passage carefully, paying attention to the changes in the pitch.

What is the difference between the functions of accent in English and Japanese? If we are able to understand this, we will be able to communicate better and convey our messages more clearly.

10–5   Variations of 'two bags' by 18 English and Japanese speakers

Japanese read the accent in each word, as you can see in the example of 'ふたつの袋' 'futatsu no fukuro' (fu**TATSU**nofu**KURO**). English speakers, on the other hand, do not. They only put emphasis on "two", not on both "two" and "bags". It is important to understand this difference.

In the case of 'two bags', the productions of English speakers and Japanese speakers of English (students) were completely different.

Japanese speakers produce an accent on each word, while English speakers produce accent only on the most important words in the sentence, not on the others.

The speech by English speakers is therefore easier to understand for the listeners, but the speech by Japanese speakers is difficult to understand because the important words are not emphasized.

10–6 'Momotaro' by Japanese and English speakers —— What are the differences?

A lot of Japanese know the story of 'Momotaro' by heart. This story is even in the Japanese textbooks in the Meiji era. I found in the preliminary experiment that 'Momotaro' is a story that people in any generation are able to read with enthusiasm and accuracy. This is because people have read the story in textbooks (beginning from 1890). I have recorded the story in more than 108 regions in Japan. I was amazed that each and every participant was a great speaker. The pitch contours had a liveliness that is similar to the English speakers' 'two bags'.

There is a clear difference with the English speakers. For instance, Japanese speakers did not read the first 'momo (peach)' in a high pitch. (English speakers would have, since this is the first time the word 'peach' appears, and thus the speaker is introducing new information, and would emphasize this with a high pitch.)

The way Japanese speakers produce important parts of the story and using accent are clearly different from that of the English speakers. The story is told in a more fascinating way by speakers above 70 years of age, compared to younger generations. The following is the original version of 'Momotaro' in Japanese, and an English translation of it.

Momotaro

Mukasi mukasi, aru tokoro ni, ojiisan to obaasanga arimasita. Ojiisanha yamahe sibakarini, obaasanha kawahe sentakuni ikimasita. Obaasanga sentakuwo siteiruto, kawakamikara ookina momoga donburako donburakoto nagaretekimasita. Obaasanha sonomomowo hirotte iehe kaerimasita.

Obaasanga momowo kiroutosuruto, momoga futatsuni warete, nakakara ookina otokonokoga umaremasita. Ojiisanto obaasanha sonokoni Momotaro toiu nawo tsukemasita.

桃太郎

　むかしむかし、あるところに、おじいさんとおばあさんがありました。おじいさんは山へしばかりに、おばあさんは川へ洗濯にいきました。

　おばあさんが洗濯をしていると、川上から大きな桃がどんぶらこどんぶらこと流れてきました。おばあさんはその桃を拾って家へ帰りました。

　おばあさんが桃を切ろうとすると、桃がふたつにわれて、中から大きな男の子が生まれました。おじいさんとおばあさんはその子に桃太郎という名をつけました。

Momotaro

Once upon a time, there lived an old man and an old woman. The old man went to the mountain to gather twigs, and the old woman went to a stream to do the washing.

When the old woman was washing clothes, she saw a big peach floating towards her on the water. She picked up the peach and went home with it.

The old man and woman cut open the peach, and found a boy inside. They named him MOMOTARO.

These two passages were compared with the recordings of readers with occupations related to education and the recordings of old generation in each region.

10–7 Intonation pattern of the reading

The intonation patterns in narrative reading have some common characteristics. If parts of speech where a lot of speakers produced a high pitch (corresponding with word accent) were capitalized, it would look something like this.

muKASImuKASI oJIisantooBAasangaaRIMAsita. oJIisanhayaMAhesiBAKARINI oBAasanhakaWAheseNTAKUNIiKIMAsita. oBAasangakaWAdeseNTAKUWOsiTEIRUTO kaWAKAMIKARAOokinamoMO(1)gaDOnburakoDOnburakotonaGAretekimasita. oBAasanhamo

MO(2)WOhiROtteiEhekaERIMAsita. moMO(3)WOWARUTONAka kara…

The 'momo (peach)' in the passage are numbered from (1) to (3), according to the number of emergence. The repeated words other than 'momo' are four 'obaasan' and two 'ojiisan'. These are all read with a high pitch. (1) 'momo' is read low (see 'momo' in Figure 1), and (2) and (3) are read with a high pitch.

(1) 'momo' is the first important word in the passage, but emphasis is on 'ookina' in 'ookina momo ga', and 'momo' is low. A majority of speakers produce 'momo' in low, short, and weak manner. (3) is at the beginning of a sentence, and is produced with a high pitch.

A lot of speakers' pitch is influenced by the position within a sentence and whether there is a preceding pause or not.

10–8 Fundamental differences of English and Japanese speakers' 'English accent'

If this story were written in English, how would English speakers read it? And how about Japanese speakers who has just read it in Japanese?

Once upon a time, there lived an old man and an old woman. The old man went to the mountain to gather twigs, and the old woman went to a stream to do the washing.

When the old <u>wo</u>man was washing <u>clothes</u>, she saw a big <u>peach</u> floating <u>towards</u> her on the <u>water</u>. She <u>picked up</u> the peach and went <u>home</u> with it.

The old man and woman <u>cut</u> open the peach, and found a <u>boy</u> in<u>side</u>. They <u>named</u> him MOMO<u>TA</u>RO.

The underlined parts are where more than three English speakers read with a high pitch. In Japanese, adjectives, adverbs, and onomatopoeic expressions tend to be emphasized. The words preceding or following them, on the contrary, are read with a rather low pitch, whether they are important in the storyline or not.

It does not mean that Japanese speakers reading the English translated version of 'Momotaro' pronounced important words clearly

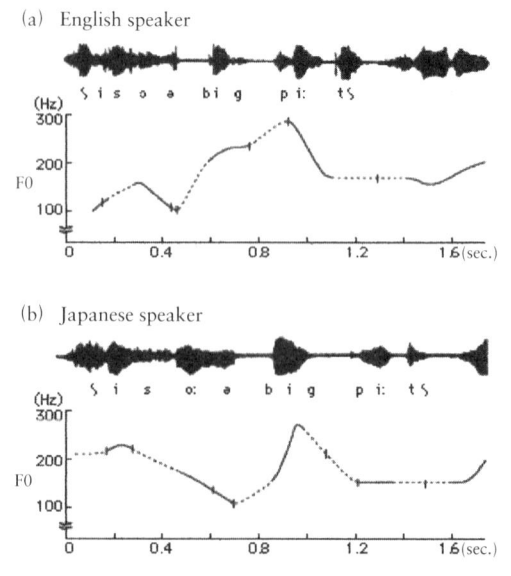

Figure 10-4 Pitch contours and waveforms of 'She saw a big peach floating'

CHAPTER 10: What is the difference between English and Japanese accent? 133

with a high pitch. For example, Japanese speakers tend to produce 'old' in 'old man' and 'old woman' with a high pitch. As in the case of Japanese 'ojiisan, obaasan', all six speakers produced 'big' in 'big peach' in a high pitch, and 'peach' in a low pitch. In English, repeated words are substituted with pronouns. So, the first occurrence of the word must be pronounced clearly and expressively. We see, thus, that speech expressions differ when linguistic rules are different.

For example, Figure 10–4 shows the sound waves and pitch contours of Japanese 'ookina momo ga donburako…' and English 'she

(a) English speaker

(b) Japanese speaker

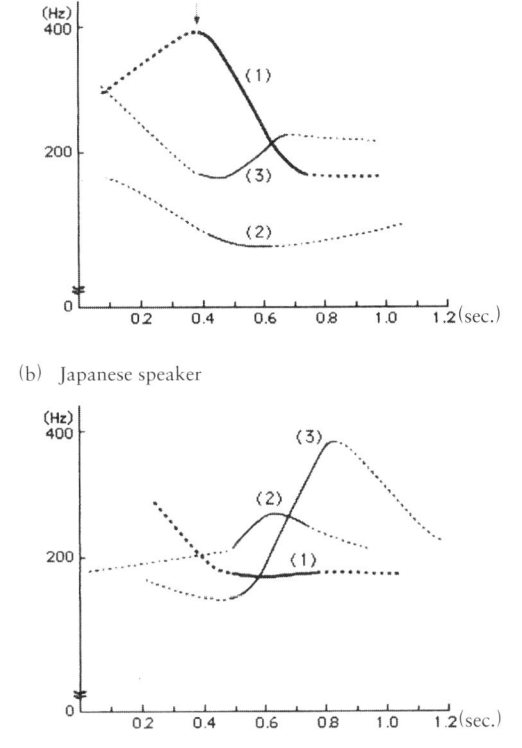

Figure 10–5 Overlapping pitch contours of 'peach' by the three speakers

saw a big peach floating…'. Let's observe the voice intensity from the sound wave amplitude, and the change in voice pitch from the pitch contour. This English speaker produces 'big' slightly high, and 'peach' especially high, but the six Japanese speakers are producing 'big' in a high pitch and 'peach' in a low pitch. The way Japanese speakers read the English passage is in the same manner as in the Japanese passage.

Figure 10–5 shows (a) English speakers' and (b) Japanese speakers' pitch contours of 'peach' overlapped. In the case of Japanese speakers, (1) 'peach' after 'big' is in a low pitch and 'peach' in (2) and (3) are in a high pitch, just as in (1) (2) (3) in the previous 'Momotaro'. This shows that the intonation of Japanese speakers' English is completely different from that of the English speakers'. This may be one of the reasons that English spoken by Japanese speakers is difficult to understand.

10–9   Application to English pronunciation teaching

In Japanese, accent positions in words are fixed. Even in sentences, the word accent is fixed and read or spoken as it is. English, on the other hand, does not have a fixed accent position. Accented syllables are read clearly with a high pitch for words that need to be emphasized. This is enough for the listeners to understand what the speaker wants to emphasize. This is a big difference in speech expression between Japanese and English accent.

It is important that students learning English are taught these problems in order to be able to produce comprehensible English for English speakers.

Epilogue

It has long been considered that Japanese has a pitch accent and English has a stress accent.

However, measurement of the sound waves of approximately 550 words each spoken by Tokyo and Osaka dialect speakers and 400 words by English speakers has revealed that accent is based on pitch and dynamic state of intonation. Acoustical analyses as well as experiments using synthesized sounds were performed, and the results showed that accent is not related to the changes in intensity, but rather perceived by the changes in pitch. Moreover, the phoniatric method, that is, using laryngeal electromyography, has proved that both Japanese and English accents are based on changes in pitch.

It is not accurate to say that accent production is based on intensity, but rather a durational change in pitch for English as well, and this was proved by phonetic physiological experiments. Joint research also made it possible to create synthesized sounds with 40 types of pitch contours, and the perceptual experiments on accent by dialectal accent speakers were carried out with high school students. The results indicated that accent perception has individual as well as dialectal differences, and the information extracted from the results may well contribute to accent education.

Japanese words consist of sound combinations and accent made by changes in pitch. It is the same for English. But in the case of English, accented syllables are produced clearly with a high pitch for words that need to be emphasized in spoken speech. This makes it easier for the listeners to comprehend. This is one of the greatest differences between English and Japanese accent.

These experiments have shown that both Japanese and English accent is based on pitch, which differs from what has been said before. The important point is that the 'function of accent' is different for the two languages. It is especially important in terms of English language education to understand the differences in the functions of accent.

English teachers must understand the differences of Japanese and English accent.

Additionally, important parts of speech must be produced clearly when talking in Japanese as well, and we should consider speaking in a way that is easy for listeners to comprehend. Then, we should reconfirm the differences in the usage of accent in English.

Consonants and vowels are produced with commands from the brain. We also change the pitch. 'Sound' and 'voice' is controlled separately, but human beings are able to produce speech continuously. Therefore, the timing of producing sounds and controlling pitch must be matched. This mystery took quite a while to solve, but it didn't take long to notice the answer. I drew many figures, nodded to myself that I had solved the problem, slept over it, and the next day I could not recall what I had come up with. But this really is the fun part of being a researcher!

Epilogue

Behind this life-long research, I could not possibly forget Professor Hisanosuke Izui of Kyoto University's words 'Let's name this dynamic measurement. This is it!'. It all began with the encounter with Mr. Saburo Uemura, research manager at SONY. Also, Professor Emeritus Tetsuya Kunihiro of University of Tokyo recommended the publication of this book. I would like to express my sincere gratitude.

The problem of Japanese education as well as English education in Japan has been a debated topic recently. Research on both languages, with patience and effort, is necessary to tackle these problems. I would be honored if this book shall make even a small contribution to them. Spoken language, unique to humans, is a deep and fascinating mystery, and I hope that its research will continue for a long, long time.

January, 2011
Miyoko Sugito

Reference

Armstrong, L. E. & Ward, I. C. (1926): *Handbook of English Intonation*. Cambridge: Heffer.

Atkinson, J. E. (1978): Correlation analysis of the physiological factors controlling fundamental voice frequency. *Journal of Acoustic Society of America* 63.

Bloch, B. & Trager, G. L. (1942): The syllabic phonemes of English, *Language* 17.

Bloomfield, L. (1933): *Language*. New York: Holt.

Bolinger, D. (1958): A theory of pitch accent in English. *World* 14.

Cheung, J. Y., Holden, A. D. C. and Minifie, F. D. (1977): Computer Recognition of linguistic stress patterns in connected speech. *IEEE Transactions on Acoustics, Speech, and Signal Processing*. June. IEEE Signal Processing Society Press: Los Alamitos. California.

Edwards, E. R. (1904) Translated by Takamatsu, Y. (1969): *Nihongono onseigakuteki kenkyu*, Kouseishakouseikaku.

Fromkin, V. & Ohala, J. (1968): Laryngeal control and a model of speech production. *UCLA Working Papers in Phonetics* No. 10.

Chiba, T. (1935): *Jikken onseigakujoukara mitaru akusentono kenkyu*, Fuzambo.

Chiba, T. & Kajiyama, M. (1942): *Vowel, Its Nature and Structure*. Translation by Sugito, M. & Honda, K. (2003): *Boin: Sono seishitu to kozo*, Iwanami Shoten.

Fry, D. B. (1955): Duration and intensity as physical correlates of linguistics. *Journal of Acoustical Society of America* 27. Acoustical Society of America: New York.

Fujimura, O. (1967): *Nihongo no onsei: Gengokeishikino onkeikijyutsukara onpamadeno michinori*, NHK Bunken Soritsu 20 shunen kinenronbunshu, NHK Publishing.

Fujimura, O. (2007): *Onseikagakugenron: Gengono honshitsu wo kangaeru*, Iwanami Shoten.

Fujisaki, H. & Sudo, H. (1971): Nihongo tango akusentono kihonshuhasu patanto sono seiseikikouno moderu, *Journal of the Acoustical Society of Japan*, 27.

Fujisaki, H., Mitsui, Y. and Sugito, M. (1974): Kinkihougenno 2 haku tango akusentono bunsekigousei oyobi chikaku, *Proceedings of the Acoustical Society of Japan*, 3–2–18.

Fujisaki, H & Sugito, M. (1976): Acoustic and perceptual analysis of word accent types in the Osaka dialect. *Annual Bulletin* 10, Research Institute of Logopedics and Phoniatrics, University of Tokyo.

Fujisaki, H., Morikawa, H. and Sugito, M. (1976): Temporal organization of articulatory and phonatory controls in realization of Japanese word accent, *Annual Bulletin* 10. Research Institute of Logopedics and Phoniatrics, University of Tokyo.

Fujisaki, H. & Sugito, M. (1977): Onsei no butsuriteki seishitsu, Iwanami kouza Nihongo 5, *Onin*, Iwanami Shoten.

Fujisaki, H. & Sugito, M. (1978): Kinkihougen tango akusentogatano bunseki oyobi chikaku, *Journal of the Acoustical Society of Japan*, 34–3.

Hattori, S. (1931–33): Kokugo shohougenno akusento gaikan, (1)–(6), *Hougen*, Vol.1 Chapters1, 3, 4, Vol. 2 Chapters 1, 4, Vol. 3 Chapter 6, Shunyodo Publishing.

Hattori, S. (1951): *Onseigaku*, Iwanami Shoten.

Hattori, S. (1960): *Gengogakuno houhou*, Iwanami Shoten.

Hirayama, T. (1940): *Zen nihon akusentono shosou*, Ikuei Shoin.

Hirayama, T. (1957): *Nihongo onchono kenkyu*, Meiji Shoin.

Hirose, H., Shimada, J. and Ohara, J. (1969): Tango akusentoni kansuru rinjokojokin no sayo, *Proceedings of the Acoustical Society of Japan*, 3-2-1.

Hirose, H. & Sawashima, M. (1979): Ei(bei)gono sutoresuni okeru koutouchousetsu, *Acoustical Society of Japan Speech Committee handout*, S79-16.

Hirose, H. (1997): Akusento intoneshonha donoyounishite tsukurareruka, *Nihongo onsei [2] Akusento Intoneshon Rizumu to Pozu*, supervised by Sugito, Sanseido.

Inoue, O. (1916): Gocho genre joron 1–6, *Kokugakuinzasshi*, Vol.22, Issues 1–4, 7–10.

Jones, D. (1909): *The Pronunciation of English*. Cambridge University Press: Cambridge.

Jones, D. (1932): *An outline of English Phonetics*. Cambridge: Heffer.

Kindaichi, H. (1943): Kokougo akusentono shiteki kenkyu, Dialectological Circle of Japan (Eds.) *Kokugo akusentono hanashi*, Shunyodo Publishing.

Kindaichi, H. (1944): Ruijyumyogishoni hodokosaretaru shofuni tsuite, *Kokugogaku ronshu*, Iwanami Shoten.

Kindaichi, H. (1967): *Nihongo onin no kenkyu*, Tokyodo Shuppan.

Kindaichi, H. (1974): *Kokugo akusentono shitekikenkyu: genrito houhou*, Hanawa Shobo.

Ladefoged, P. (1962): Subglottal activity during speech. *Proceedings IVth International Congress of Phonetic Sciences*. Mouton, the Hague.

Lehiste, I. & Peterson, G. E. (1958): Vowel amplitude and phonemic stress in American English. *Ann. Arbor*, Michigan: Speech Research Laboratory. University of Michigan.

Liberman, A. M. & Cooper, F. S. (1962): A motor theory of speech perception. *Proceedings. Speech Communication Seminar*, Stockholm.

Liberman, P. (1967): *Intonation, Perception, and Language*. MIT Press: Massachusetts Cambridge.

Lindblom, B. (1963): Spectrographic study of vowel reduction. *Journal of Acoustic Society of America 35*. Acostical Society of America: New York.

Mattingly, I. (1966): Synthesis by rule of prosodic features. *Language and Speech 9*.

Meyer, E. A. (1906): Der musikalishe Wortakzent im Japanischen. *Le Monde Oriental, Uppsala University*. pp. 77–86.

Murayama, S. (Translated) (1976): Polivanov, E.D. *Nihongo kenkyu*, Koubundou.

Nakatani, L.H. & Aston, C. H. (1979): *Acoustic and linguistic factors in stress perception*. Bell Laboratories, 07974: New Jersey.

Neustupný, J. V. (1966): Is the Japanese accent a pitch accent?, *Onseigakkai kaiho*, 121.

Öhman, S. (1967): Word and sentence intonation, a quantitative model. *QPSR* 2–3. Royal Institute of Technology.

Palmer, H. E. & Blandford, W. G. (1924): *A Grammar of Spoken English on a Strictly Phonetic Basis*. Cambridge: Heffer.

Polivanov, E.D., Translation by Murayama, S. (1976): Nishinihongono ongakuteki akusento, *Nihongo kenkyu*, Koubundou.

Поливанов, Е. Д. (1928): *Введение в Языкознание для Востоковедных Вузов*. Ленинград.

Sakuma, K. (1929): *Onseino kenkyu*, Bungakusha.

Stevens. K. N. (1960): Toward a model for speech recognition, *Journal of Acoustic Society of America* 32.

Sugito, M. (1965): Shibatasan to Imadasan: Tangono chokakuteki benbetsuni tsuiteno ichikousatsu, *Gengo seikatsu*, 40–6.

Sugito, M. (1969): Doutaisokuteiniyoru nihongo akusentono kaimei, *Gengo kenkyu*, 55.

Sugito, M. (1970): Nihongo boinno doutaisokuteito akusentono ninshiki, *Onseikagaku kenkyu*, V.

Sugito, M. (1971): Museihakuto akusentono mondai, *handout distributed at the 64th Meeting of the Linguistic Society of Japan*.

Sugito, M. (1972): Hanakago hana kago to sakuragasakukou: Doutaisokuteiniyoru nihongoakusentono kenkyu, *Osaka Shoin Joshi Daigaku Ronshu*, Vol.10.

Sugito, M. & Fujisaki, H. (1976): *Accentual characteristics of one-and two-mora words in the Osaka dialect*. Presentation handout distributed at World Phoneticians Meeting, Sophia University.

Sugito, M. & Hirose, H. (1978): An electromyographic study of the Kinki accent, *Annual Bulletin* 12. Research Institute of Logopedics and Phoniatrics, University of Tokyo. pp.35–51.

Sugito, M. (1980): Ososagari kou: Doutaisokuteiniyoru nihongo akusentono kenkyu, Tokugawa, M. (Eds.), *Ronshu nihongo kenkyu 2: Akusento*, Yuseido Shuppan.

Sugito, M. & Fujisaki, H. (1980): Hougen washaniokeru akusentono seiseito chikaku, *Proceedings of the Acoustical Society of Japan*, 1–6–16.

Sugito, M. (1980): Akusento intoneshonno hikaku, *Nichieigo hikaku koza I: Onseito keitai*, Kunihiro, T. (Ed.), Taishukan Shoten.

Sugito, M. (1982): *Nihongo akusentono kenkyu*, Sanseido.

Sugito, M. (1994): *An overview of studies on Japanese prosody,* Study of Sounds 23, pp.227–271, Phonetic Society of Japan.

Sugito, M. (1995, 1996a): *Osaka Tokyo akusento onsei jiten CD-ROM*, Maruzen.

Sugito, M. (1996b): *Nihongo onseino kenkyu 2: Nihonjinno eigo*, Izumi Shoin.

Sugito, M. (1996c): *SUGI Speech Analizer*, Animo.

Sugito, M. (2003): Timing Relationships between Prosodic and Segmental Control in Osaka Japanese Word Accent, *Phonetica* 60 (1), pp. 1–16. Karger AG: Basel.

Sugito, M. (2005): Zen nihonno 105 chiten to 13 toshi 5 setaino washaniyoru hougen onseino shutaisei: DVD Nihongo onsei detabesu, *Nihongono kenkyu*, Vol.2, Issue 2, The Society for

Japanese Linguistics.

Sugito, M. & Kakehi, K. (2005): DVD: Nihongo onsei detabesu no kansei, *Onsei kenkyu*, 9–3.

Sugito, M. (2005): Nyuyojito hahaoyatono taiwa onsei detabesu: Emi-chan, *Onsei kenkyu*, 9–3.

Sawashima, M., Hirose, H., Honda, K. and Sugito, M. (1980): Choonto oncho seigyono jikanteki kanrennituite 2 haku muimigoniokeru shoken, *Proceedings of the Acoustical Society of Japan*, 1–6–5.

Tokugawa, M. (Ed.) (1980): *Ronshu nihongo kenkyu 2: Akusento*, Yuseido Shuppan.

Trager, G. L. & Smith, H. L. (1951): *An Outline of English Structure, Norman*. Battenburg Press: Oklahoma.

Wada, M. (1947): Akusentogata kan hyogenhou, *Kikan kokugo*, Showa 22 Autumn issue.

Yamada, T. (Bimyo) (1892): *Nihon daijiten*, Meihodo.

NHK Nihongo hatsuon akusento jiten New Edition (1998), NHK Publishing.

Naso (1516) Gonaraingyosen.

Ruijyumyogisho (1100?), Kanchiinhon (Revised 1251).

DVD: Nihongo onsei detabesu (2005) Nagoya Industrial Science Research Institute Chubu Technology Licensing Office.

INDEX

a

accent   3, 58, 72, 73
accent on voiceless mora   51, 65
accent patterns   31
accent perception   48, 77, 87, 92, 115
accent production   94
accent production model   85
accent regions   92
accent symbol   29, 60
accent types   78, 92
accented devoiced mora   17
acoustics   47
alphabet   26
alveolar ridge   24
analysis software   37
Analysis-by Synthesis   48
articulatory reference theory   48
automatic speech recognition   47

b

Bolinger   46, 115

c

compound word   44
consonants   10, 13, 23
contour boundaries   87

Cricothyroid   96
CT   96, 99, 113

d

Densuke   xxvii, 61, 75
dialectal accent   92
dialects   3
duration   46, 70

e

E. A. Meyer   57
education of speech   22
emphasis   123
English accent   68, 69, 89, 103, 106, 117
English Japanese native speakers   117
English learners   127
English pronunciation teaching   134
English speakers   118

f

falling accent pattern   34
falling intonation   45
falling pitch   56, 60, 66, 79
following mora   62
fricative   10
Fry   46
fundamental frequency (F0)   38
fundamental frequency contours   83, 85

g

geminate   15

h

hard palate　8
Heian era　30, 36
high-low accent　41, 45
high-starting　106
historical and geographical correspondence　30
historical and regional patterns　58

i

infants　44
instructions of reading aloud　124
intonation　4, 130

j

Japanese accent　117
Japanese education　22
Japanese English learner　26, 124
Japanese native speakers　26, 119
Japanese syllabary　21

k

Kagoshima　33
Kanae Sakuma　51
Kansai accent　3, 31, 33, 36, 40, 62, 89, 103, 104, 106, 112, 116, 120
Kansai dialect　50, 53, 61, 68, 84, 99
Kenji Miyazawa　15
Kochi accent　36

l

labial sound　24

laryngeal electromyogram　105
laryngeal electromyography　96, 101, 112
late fall　49, 51, 56, 66, 78
Lateral Cricoarytenoid　96
LCA　99
lengthening　15
lexicon classification　30
low-beginning　104
lowering of the voice　104, 113

m

Masato Kajiyama　49
Miemura　57
model for speech mechanism　48
Momotaro　128
monophthongs　26
mora　13, 19, 117
MRI　5
musical perception　92

n

nasals　10
Naso　23
Neustupný　50
no accent region　91
no-accent type　35, 94

o

Öhman　48, 83
on/off commands　101
open-reel　xxxi
oscilocoda　xxv

p

palate 8
pause 13
Pen-oscillo xxix
perception of accent 46
perceptual experiment 65, 89, 91
phonation duration 17
pitch accent 49, 62, 115
pitch contour 39, 68, 82, 83, 110, 111
place of articulation 24
plosives 10
produce accent 109
Production model of Japanese accent 105

r

regional differences 92
rhythm 13, 16, 69
rise in the voice pitch 101
rising intonation 41
rising pitch 55
Ruijuumyougishou 30, 60

s

Sanskrit 21
SH 96, 99, 113
Shuntaro Tanigawa 11
soft palate (velum) 8
SONY laboratory xxv
sound wave xxix, 37, 39, 75
spectrograms 113
speech analysis 47
speech synthesis 47
speech training 22
starting point of fall voice pitch 112

Sternohyoid 96
stress 115
stress accent 41, 45, 67
subglottal pressure 103
syllabic nasal 15
syllable 19, 118
symbols accent 24
synthesized English sounds 115
synthesized sound 80, 81
synthesized speech xxv, 61

t

Tales of Heike 15
teaching accent 90
throat 1
timing 112
Tokyo 33
Tokyo accent 3, 17, 33, 37, 38, 40, 89, 100, 106, 116, 120
Tokyo dialect 30, 50
Tsutomu Chiba 49

v

vocal folds 2, 4
vocal organs 7
vocal tract 4
voice 1
voice pitch 41
voiced consonant 10, 52, 55
voiceless consonants 10, 55
voiceless mora 67, 109
vowel 4, 13
vowel devoicing 10, 53
word accent 44, 76, 101, 115
word sentences 76

【著者紹介】

杉藤美代子（すぎとう みよこ）

東京都出身。1941年、東京女子高等師範学校（現、お茶の水女子大学）文科卒業。京都大学文学部言語学科故泉井久之助教授の指導を受ける。文学博士（東京大学）。元大阪樟蔭女子大学名誉教授。元日本音声学会会長。2012年2月、没。

（主な編著書）
『日本語アクセントの研究』（1982　三省堂）
『日本人の声（日本語音声の研究1）』（1994　和泉書院）
『東京・大阪アクセント音声辞典CD-ROM』（1995　丸善）
『声に出して読もう！―朗読を科学する―』（1996　明治書院）
『音声文法』（編）（2011　くろしお出版）

【訳者】　増田斐那子　早稲田大学助教
【監修者】　ドナ・エリクソン　上智大学・金沢医科大学非常勤講師

Word Accent in Japanese and English
What Are the Differences?

日本語のアクセント、英語のアクセント　どこがどう違うのか（日本版タイトル）

発行	2014年5月16日　初版1刷
定価	2200円＋税
著者	© 杉藤美代子
訳者	増田斐那子
監修者	ドナ・エリクソン
発行者	松本功
装丁者	渡部文
印刷・製本所	三美印刷株式会社
発行所	株式会社 ひつじ書房
	〒112-0011 東京都文京区千石2-1-2 大和ビル2F
	Tel.03-5319-4916　Fax.03-5319-4917
	郵便振替 00120-8-142852
	toiawase@hituzi.co.jp　http://www.hituzi.co.jp/

ISBN978-4-89476-720-1　C3080

造本には充分注意しておりますが、落丁・乱丁などがございましたら、小社かお買上げ書店にておとりかえいたします。ご意見、ご感想など、小社までお寄せ下されば幸いです。